THE HOME BOOK OF
SCOTTISH COOKERY

D0994103

THE HOME BOOK OF
SCOTTISH COOKERY

Aileen King and Fiona Dunnett

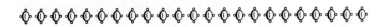

FABER & FABER

First published in May 1967 by
Faber and Faber Limited
3 Queen Square London WC1
First published in this edition 1973
Printed in Great Britain by
Whitstable Litho Straker Brothers Ltd
All rights reserved

ISBN 0 571 10332 4 (Faber Paper Covered Editions)

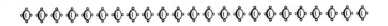

CONTENTS

HOME COOKING IN SCOTLAND

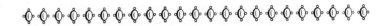

There is no more fruitful line of investigation in the
world at present, than the combination between
farmers and scientists in Scotland. WALTER ELLIOT

Scotland is the best place in the world to make an
appetite. H. V. MORTON

Home cooking has changed in Scotland as it has everywhere
else during the last few decades, and in some homes there is
little difference in fare from anywhere else in the British Isles.
But the Scots housewife is supreme in certain branches of
cookery and these are the traditional dishes, good plain
wholesome food for which the country has always been
famous. There has always been an abundance of fish and
game and the staple bread has been provided by oats and
barley, both of which grow well. By the twelfth century,
fishing was one of the most important industries on both east
and west coasts, and sheep and cattle were kept on most
holdings. The hardy cattle, both Galloway and Highland,
supplied milk for butter and cheese and the sheep were valued
for their wool. The people were not great meat eaters but
used the carcases of beef and mutton for broths, soups and
stews. After the evictions and consequent loss of their plots of
land, country people used wild vegetables in place of the
roots and kail they had been accustomed to cultivate. The
potato came to Scotland from Ireland early in the eighteenth
century, about the time when the great development in
gardening was beginning.

7

In early times, in spite of periods of intense poverty due to invasion and also clan warfare, the common people fared as well as anywhere in Europe. Their methods of cooking were simple, relying upon the kail-pot, the bakestone and the brander or gridiron; all used over a peat fire, hence the characteristic broths and soups, grilled and smoked fish and bannocks. Before the industrial revolution, most of Scotland was sparsely populated, and even before the evictions there was a meagre sufficiency of food for everyone. The important grain crop, oats, is, in many an expert's opinion, the reason for the physical and mental energy of the Scot. Apprentices and students were said to live mainly on oatmeal, sometimes moistened with bree, and students were granted a day's holiday, known as Meal Monday, half-way through the University term, in order that they might go home to replenish their bag of meal. Many were very ill-nourished and suffered accordingly. The best of the barley went and still goes to the brewer, the next best to the distiller and the remainder to the mill.

In addition to the homely recipes for using game, fish and oatmeal on which the traditional dishes of the ordinary homes are built, the country owes much to the influence of the French who came over during the long period of the Auld Alliance. Names of dishes and cooking terms still used are often derived from the French. By the sixteenth century, the highly civilized customs of France had been introduced into Scotland, to Edinburgh in particular, by the entourage of the French nobles who came over whenever there was an alliance between the royal houses of Scotland and France.

Mary of Lorraine and Guise, the wife of James V and mother of Mary Stuart, was responsible for setting the lead in elaborate entertaining in the French manner and there was much extravagant banqueting. This led eventually to genuine food shortages for the ordinary people and John Knox rebuked people for high living. In 1581, a law was passed against 'superfluous banqueting' and dishes were regulated according to rank except on feast days and holi-

8

days. The aristocratic houses served their food in the French manner with wines imported from France, followed by brandy. The Scottish people drank ale, especially in the Lowlands, and most housewives made wine from the flowers and fruits of the hedgerows.

During the eighteenth century, the knowledge of crop husbandry and improved methods of agriculture and horticulture were used in Scotland and better and more varied vegetables than the cabbage, kail and potato were grown. Although the climate can be rigorous and the harvests uncertain, there are large tracts of land as fertile as any in the United Kingdom where some of the world's best beef, potatoes and poultry are produced. Rich pastureland in the lowlands feeds dairy cows such as Ayrshires which give rich milk, and excellent butter and cheese are produced. Wild berries of raspberries, strawberries and gooseberries were the forerunner of the varieties for which the country is now famous. The wild varieties like the blaeberry are still used, to produce some of the well-known traditional preserves and puddings.

But the great fame of the Scottish housewife is her baking and the results of her skill are best seen at breakfast and tea. This is especially true in the country areas where local-grown produce is served with the scones, cakes and breads. Members of the family now often take a canteen or a school meal at midday and want to be out in the evening on activities outside the home. Thus a meal between 5.30 p.m. and 6.30 p.m. is convenient and so high tea is once more in vogue. The fashion for afternoon tea, introduced during the seventeenth century, spurred on the Scottish housewife to develop her skills with girdle and oven. Until the 1880's tea was always taken at home, it being a strictly feminine occasion, and the men foregathered at the coffee houses. Then Miss Cranston, the daughter of a Glasgow hotel owner, introduced tearooms to Glasgow and this was the start of the habit of taking tea in a café. Both amateur and professional baking reached the high standard which is still maintained.

It is interesting to note that in Scotland 'a good cook' is not necessarily the same thing as 'a good baker' and the latter attribute is the more highly prized.

Many of the really old family recipes are difficult to follow today and the following collection includes what are felt to be the best of the regional dishes. The recipes have been adapted and adjusted so that they can be made in an ordinary kitchen by an ordinary housewife, using the commodities available in the shops and markets. Unless otherwise stated all quantities are for four persons.

OVEN TEMPERATURES

Manufacturers of gas cookers do not show temperatures on the thermostats of gas ovens but use numbers—in most cases the range is $\frac{1}{4}$ to 9—to indicate the heat of the oven. The temperature corresponding to a number does not vary to any marked extent between one make of cooker and another and the following are the temperatures in the centre of the oven equivalent to the numbers on the thermostat.

$\frac{1}{4}$–$\frac{1}{2}$	245°–270° F	very cool oven
1	290° F	cool oven
2	315° F	cool oven
3	335° F	warm oven
4	365° F	moderate oven
5	385° F	fairly hot oven
6	405° F	hot oven
7	425° F	hot oven
7–8	425°–445° F	hot–very hot oven
8	445° F	very hot oven
9	470° F +	very hot oven

Always use the book of instructions given with each cooker as temperatures within the oven vary. In the book indications of this fact are given.

Soups

SOUPS

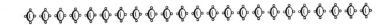

Good soup is the first course of the midday meal in many Scottish homes. The Scots housewife is prepared to take trouble to make a good stock from bones and root vegetables and this is the foundation of the good flavour. The young, busy housewife may turn to a bouillon cube for the base of her soup in order to save time.

The traditional soups, Cock-a-leekie, Feather Fowlie, Kail Brose, Lentil, Powsowdie and Scotch Broth are superb dishes in themselves; they are full of both flavour and nourishment. They are sometimes served to take the edge off appetite, otherwise they may be served as a course complete in itself.

There are also some delicately flavoured soups such as Lorraine, Onion and Sorrel, which owe their origin to French influence.

Some of the local recipes differ from one source to another. Each Highland cook seems to have her own mixture of ingredients for Game Soup and there are many recipes for the shellfish soups of the Hebrides and Cullen Skink from the shores of the Moray Firth.

'Broth' can mean any mixture of available vegetables, bones of meat, rabbit, game or fish, combined according to skills handed down from mother to daughter and flavoured 'to taste'.

COCK-A-LEEKIE

1 *old fowl or cock*   4 *pints water*
6 *leeks*   2 *teasp. salt*
giblets from the fowl 8 *white peppercorns*
chopped parsley to garnish

Wash the bird well, truss; put into a large pan with a well-fitting lid.

Wash the giblets and with them add the cold water, which should just cover the bird.

Add the seasonings which should be adjusted according to taste.

Prepare the leeks, discarding the very coarse outer leaves.

Wash very well, and cut up into small pieces.

Add to the bird, bring the mixture slowly to the boil. Skim well.

Cook very slowly until the legs of the bird are tender. This will vary from 2–6 hours according to the age and size of the bird.

Remove the bird and the giblets, test the soup for seasoning and skim off excess grease with kitchen paper.

Some recipes add 12 soaked prunes about 30 minutes before serving. This gives a sweet taste.

Others add 2 tablespoons of rice with the leeks.

Some recipes serve the soup, garnished with chopped parsley, and offer the bird, coated with hard-boiled egg or caper sauce, at a separate meal.

Other recipes suggest removing the meat from the carcase, cutting it up and serving it as part of the soup.

CULLEN SKINK

1 *Findon haddock*   1 *pint milk*
1 *onion peeled and chopped* *mashed potato (approx. 1 lb.)*
1 *oz. butter*   *seasoning*

Remove the skin of the haddock.

Wash and put in a pan with sufficient water to cover.

Add the onion, chopped.

Cook slowly until the haddock flesh looks creamy.

Remove the fish and separate the bones and flesh.

Put the bones back into the stock and cook for 1 hour. Strain.

To the strained stock add the flaked fish, 1 pint of milk and seasoning to taste.

Boil up and add enough mashed potato to make the soup a purée consistency.

Add the butter in small pieces with the potato.

FEATHER FOWLIE

1 *roasting chicken*	1 *sprig thyme*
1 *slice lean ham*	1 *blade mace*
1 *onion*	3 *pints water*
1 *stick celery*	3 *egg yolks*
1 *small carrot*	2 *tbs. cream from top of milk*
1 *tbs. chopped parsley*	*salt to taste*

Skin and joint the chicken, soak in salted water for 30 minutes. Drain and wash.

Put into a stewpan with the ham, the sliced vegetables, thyme, mace, parsley stalks and water. Season.

Simmer gently for 1½–2 hours until the bird is tender. Strain into a clean pan.

Remove any grease, add the meat from the fowl, minced. Heat for 15 minutes.

Add extra white stock if necessary during this time.

Draw the pan aside, add the beaten egg yolks and the cream and stir carefully into the soup. Heat to cook the eggs slightly but do not boil.

Test the seasoning.

Add the parsley just before serving.

Some people add only the white part of the meat and serve the rest as a separate dish.

GAME SOUP
Adapted from Meg Dod's Recipe

Skin game birds, rabbit, hare or venison.

Cut meat into small pieces and fry in dripping with pieces of ham, onion, carrot and parsnip.

Drain off any extra fat, add brown stock to cover and any bones and seasoning. (She suggests black pepper, cloves and salt.)

Stew for 2 hours at least. Meg Dod says 1 hour but this is much too short a time to get the full flavour from the ingredients.

Remove the bones and skim any fat from the surface and serve very hot.

This is successful if made from the remains of cooked game. Trimmings of raw venison much enrich the flavour. If small steaks of venison are cooked in the broth, they may be served separately with mashed potatoes and rowan jelly.

HOTCH POTCH

½ *lb. neck of lamb*
3 *new carrots*
2 *new turnips*
½ *small cauliflower*
4 *oz. shelled peas*
4 *oz. broad beans*

4 *syboes (spring onions)*
4 *leaves lettuce or cabbage*
1 *tbs. chopped parsley*
1 *qt. water*
salt, pepper
1 *level teasp. sugar*

18

Wash the meat and put into a pan with cold water and salt. Bring to the boil and skim if necessary. Add pepper. Simmer 1½–2 hours. Prepare the vegetables according to kind. Dice the carrot and turnip, divide the cauliflower into small sprigs, remove the skin from the beans, slice the syboes and shred the lettuce or cabbage. Add to the pan all the vegetables except the lettuce and peas and simmer 30–40 minutes. Add the lettuce and peas and simmer 10 minutes. Remove the meat, cut in dice and return to the pan or serve separately. Add the parsley and sugar, correct the seasoning and dish.

This is essentially a summer soup, making use of tender, young vegetables. It should be very thick.

KAIL BROSE

There are dozens of recipes for this dish but they are all virtually curly kail shredded or chopped, cooked in stock and thickened with oatmeal, barley or rice. Some recipes just say 'Stock', others direct that cow heel, or rabbit or belly pork shall be used. Some add carrot, turnip and onion—some leave these in the soup after the kail is added, others demand a strained stock in which the kail is cooked and to which 1 tablespoon oatmeal or 1 teaspoon barley per person is added half an hour before the kail.

This is a sound, basic recipe:

1 *lb. green kail*
seasoning
3 *pints good stock made according*   1 *oz. barley or* 2 *oz. oatmeal*
  to preference in flavour or
  available ingredients

Cook the oatmeal or barley in the stock for half an hour. Add shredded, washed kail and cook for another half-hour. Season and serve with oatcakes.

LENTIL SOUP

6 *oz. lentils*
1 *carrot, onion, potato and stick*
   of celery
¼ *pint milk*

2 *pints water*
1 *ham bone*
seasoning

Put the lentils, chopped carrot, onion, celery and potato into the pan. Add the water, ham bone and seasoning.
   Cook for 2 hours at simmering point. Stir occasionally.
   Remove the ham bone, sieve, or put in liquidizer.
   Boil up with the milk and correct the seasoning.
   Serve with toast croûtons.

LORRAINE SOUP

3 *pints good white stock*
1 *lb. cooked, minced white meat*
   (*veal, chicken, rabbit or a*
   mixture)
2 *oz. blanched almonds*

2 *hard-boiled egg yolks, sieved*
1 *tbs. fine white crumbs*
seasonings
¼ *pint cream or top of milk*
1 *tbs. chopped parsley*

Mix the almonds, egg yolks and minced meat in a liquidizer or rub through a mouli.
   Heat the crumbs in a little stock and add to the pounded mixture. Add the remainder of the stock.
   Season with salt and pepper, powdered mace and lemon juice to taste. Boil. Remove from the heat, stir in the cream and reheat, but do not boil.
   Garnish with chopped parsley.

ONION SOUP

1 lb. onions chopped

2 oz. butter

½ oz. cornflour

¼ teasp. mustard

2 pints brown stock

1 teasp. salt

black pepper to taste

Fry the onions in the butter until a rich brown. This will take about 15 minutes.

Add the stock and the seasonings.

Cook at simmering point for 1½ hours.

Mix the cornflour with the stock or water.

Add to the soup and boil for 5 minutes.

This may be served the French way by putting a round of toast thickly spread with grated cheese in each soup bowl and pouring the soup over.

PARTAN BREE (Crab Soup)

1 cooked crab

3 oz. rice

1–2 teasp. salt

⅛ teasp. white pepper

1 pint white stock

1 pint milk

2–3 teasp. anchovy essence

¼ pint thin cream

Boil the rice in the milk until soft and creamy.

Mix in the crab meat, reserving what is taken from the claws.

Sieve, or put into a liquidizer until absolutely smooth and creamy.

Add white stock as necessary until the mixture is like the consistency of thin cream.

Test and adjust the seasoning, adding the anchovy essence.

Heat thoroughly, add the meat from the claws, and the cream.

Re-test the seasoning and reheat, but do not reboil.

POTATO SOUP

1 *lb. potatoes*	2 *pints water*
½ *lb. carrots*	1 *onion*
1 *large bone*	*salt, pepper*

Wash the bone, peel the onion and put in a pan with the water and seasoning.

Bring to the boil and simmer 1 hour.

After peeling, cut the potatoes into even-sized dice and grate the carrot, using a coarse mesh. Add to the stock.

Simmer 1 hour.

Remove the bone and onion, taste and correct the seasoning before serving.

POWSOWDIE or SHEEP'S HEAD BROTH

1 *sheep's head, prepared and split*	2 *oz. pearl barley*
1 *lb. mixed vegetables diced*	5–6 *pints water*
(carrot, turnip, celery, leeks)	*salt and pepper*
¼ *lb. chopped onion*	1 *tbs. chopped parsley to garnish*

Wash and soak the head.

Remove the brains and put aside in a basin with a little vinegar. Put the head, barley, 1 teaspoon salt, ⅛ teaspoon pepper and enough water to cover in a pan.

Bring to the boil, skim and simmer for 1½ hours. Add the diced vegetables and chopped onion. Simmer for a further 1½ hours. Cook longer if the head is from an old sheep. Remove the head and add the chopped parsley to the broth.

To serve the meat: Slice the meat from the head. Skin and slice the tongue. Make a good parsley sauce with ½ milk and ½ broth liquor. Add the cooked, chopped brains.

Coat the meat with the sauce and serve as a separate dish.

Note: To cook the brains, simmer 10 minutes in water. Drain and chop.

SCOTCH BROTH

1 lb. neck of mutton or lean stewing beef	1 oz. pearl barley
1 lb. diced vegetables (carrot, turnip and leek)	2 oz. soaked, dried peas
	1 teasp. salt
	¼ teasp. pepper
1 grated carrot	1 tbs. chopped parsley
3 pints cold water	4 tbs. chopped kail

The meat may be left as one piece to serve as a separate course or finely diced to serve in the soup.

Bones are cooked in the soup.

Put the meat, water, salt, pepper and washed pearl barley and peas into a pan. Bring to the boil and skim.

Add the diced vegetables and simmer 3–4 hours.

Remove the bones and the meat if it is to be served separately.

Remove excess grease and add the grated carrot and the chopped kail.

Cook a further 10 minutes.

Add the chopped parsley and reheat.

SKINK SOUP

¾ lb. hough	1 stick celery
1 oz. dripping	bouquet garni
1 onion	2 level teasp. salt
1 qt. water	¼ level teasp. pepper

Thickening:
  1 oz sago, tapioca, cornflour or flour to 1 qt. soup.

Wash the meat quickly and cut into small pieces. Melt the dripping and fry the meat till brown. Draw to one side of the pan. Slice the onion and fry till brown. Add the water and salt and bring to the boil. Skim, add the celery, bouquet garni, and pepper and simmer 3–4 hours. Strain. Thicken by sprinkling in the sago or tapioca and simmer for 10 minutes. If using cornflour or flour blend with stock or water and add to the soup. Stir till boiling and simmer till cooked. Cut the meat very finely and return to the soup.

If there is marrow in the bone, remove that and use for frying the meat instead of dripping. Add the bone to the soup before simmering.

½ lb. boneless meat is sufficient.

This soup, if accompanied by a dish of boiled potatoes, will constitute a main dish in itself.

SORREL SOUP (Mary, Queen of Scots Soup)

½ lb. sorrel leaves
2 oz. butter
3 pints white stock
¼ pint cream or top of milk

½ lb. grated potato
2 teasp. salt
⅛ teasp. white pepper

Wash and pick over the sorrel, remove any tough stalks or veins.

Melt the butter and sweat the sorrel in it until the leaves wilt.
Add the stock, salt and the grated potato.
Simmer for 1 hour. Sieve or liquidize.
Reheat in a clean pan.
Add the pepper. Taste and correct the seasoning.
Add the cream and reheat but do not reboil.
It may be garnished with whipped cream when served in hot soup cups.

STOCK

2 *lb. shin of beef, or* 3 *lb. beef*
   bones chopped
1 *small carrot*
1 *onion*
1 *piece of turnip*

1 *stick celery or* 1 *teasp. celery*
   seed
1 *teasp. salt*
6 *black and* 6 *white peppercorns*

Remove any fat from the meat and bones. Wash well.

Scoop out the marrow and use this to fry the cut-up meat and bones until they are a brown colour.

If there is no marrow, use ½ oz. dripping.

Add the water, bring slowly to the boil and skim.

Add the vegetables, peeled and cut up roughly, and the seasoning.

Simmer for 3–4 hours in an ordinary saucepan, or cook in a pressure cooker for 25 minutes.

Strain through a nylon sieve or muslin.

Cool quickly and remove the fat when cold.

Store in a cool larder or refrigerator and use within a couple of days.

STOCK FOR LIGHT COLOURED SOUPS

2 *lb. knuckle of veal or* 3 *lb.*
   bones only
1 *onion peeled*
6 *white peppercorns*

4 *pints water*
1 *teasp. salt*
1 *stick celery*

Remove any fat from the meat and bones.

Wash the bones well.

Remove marrow and discard.

Put all the ingredients into a pan and add the water.

Bring slowly to the boil. Skim well.

Simmer for 5 hours or cook in a pressure cooker for 45 minutes.

Strain carefully, cool quickly and when cold remove all traces of fat.

Fish Dishes

FISH DISHES

Meg Dod in 1826 advised the housewife that 'an eye of some experience and the sense of smell best determine the freshness of fish'. In spite of improved transport and methods of distribution this is still the soundest method of ensuring fresh and therefore well-flavoured fish such as is available in most parts of Scotland.

The Scots began to develop their vast natural fisheries in the eleventh century when the Roman Catholic Church practices became universal in Scotland. Until then, the Celtic Church had forbidden fish to be used as a food.

There is an abundance of fish in rivers and lochs as well as in the seas bordering the coast and fish of all kinds is readily available in prime condition: many an incomer to Scotland finds the local fish, however humble a variety, to be a gourmet's delight.

Herrings, fresh, salted or smoked, used to be a staple food and still the Loch Fyne herrings are much sought after. Haddock, too, are plentiful and are sold fresh or cured. This fish is found mostly on the east coast and the cured fish are known according to the local cure, each of which has its own characteristics.

The fish caught and cured in the Moray Firth are pale in colour and mild in flavour; those in Arbroath, the smokies, are stronger in flavour and are cured whole. The Findon or Finnan haddock takes its name from the village in Kincardineshire and is split and cleaned before curing. It is a golden yellow when finished. This fish is clearly distinguishable from the coloured smoked fish of indeterminate origin often seen on the fishmonger's slab.

Before improved transport encouraged their export, salmon and shell fish were eaten by the upper classes and the workers alike, in fact, as late as a century ago workers who 'lived in' stipulated that they should be given salmon no oftener than twice a week. Salmon and sea or salmon trout are served throughout the season more frequently than in most parts of the United Kingdom. The smaller sea trout are especially succulent and delicate in flavour and are not as expensive to buy as the more renowned salmon.

FLOUNDERS OR FLUKIES

Allow 1 fish weighing about ¾–1 lb. per person.

Clean, remove head, tail and fins and rub all over with salt.

Wash and dry and dip in seasoned flour.

Fry in shallow fat on both sides until golden brown.

Drain on absorbent paper and serve with sprigs of parsley and pieces of lemon.

The flounders may be cooked in deep fat. If oil is used in the deep fat pan, cook for 5–6 minutes at 330° F. Dripping or lard should show a very faint haze when the fish is put in. Cook till brown.

FRESH FILLETS
(*Haddock, whiting, plaice and sole*)

Choose fillets suitable in size for serving to one person.

Wash and dry quickly, season with salt and pepper and put into a greased shallow pan.

Add enough water, milk or a mixture of the two to cover.

Add a sprig of thyme, a small piece of mace and a small piece of bay leaf to each fillet.

Bring slowly to boiling point with the lid on; stand for 10 minutes in a warm place.

Drain, put on a hot plate with a nut of butter and a sprig of parsley to each fillet.

If liked, thicken the liquor with cornflour and serve as a sauce.

HADDOCK IN BROWN SAUCE

Take a whole fish of a suitable size allowing 6–8 oz. fish per person.

Clean, remove the head and fins, skin and cut into suitable sized pieces. Flour the pieces of fish.

Boil the trimmings with an onion and some herbs for 10–20 minutes. Strain and use the liquor for the sauce.

Fry the pieces of fish in butter until brown on both sides. Lay aside.

Make a brown roux with the remains of the butter and a tablespoon of flour. Add enough stock to make a pouring sauce. Flavour with ground mace, cinnamon and mushroom ketchup. Boil up and skim. Add the pieces of fish and cook for a few minutes until tender. The sauce should be strong in flavour, thick and smooth.

FINNAN HADDOCK—TO POACH

Put the fish, skin side up, under the grill for 1–2 minutes to shrink the skin. Peel off.

Trim off the tail and fins.

Cut the haddock into 4 pieces or 6 if the fish is very large.

Cover with a mixture of milk and water and a knob of butter.

Bring to the boil and allow to stand covered in a warm place for 5 minutes.

Drain and serve *either* with a dab of butter on each portion *or* with a poached egg on each piece of fish *or* with a sauce made by thickening the milk and water with cornflour.

Do not add salt when cooking but test the sauce before serving.

When the fish is served coated with the sauce, the dish may be garnished with chopped or sliced hard-boiled egg and/or chopped parsley.

TO GRILL FINNAN HADDOCK

Brush the portions of finnan haddock with melted butter or oil and grill for 3–5 minutes on both sides.

Serve skin side down, garnished with a dab of butter or a sprig of parsley or a pat of parsley butter.

Grilled haddock may be accompanied by grilled rashers of bacon to make a substantial high tea or supper dish.

SMOKIES

Remove the head and the tail.

Place in a frying-pan with about $\frac{1}{2}''$ water in it.

Bring to the boil slowly and keep the pan closely covered.

Drain and serve with pats of butter.

HERRINGS FRIED IN OATMEAL

(a) *Whole Fish*

Clean the herring and cut off the head and fins. Dry.

Toss in seasoned oatmeal and fry in hot dripping until brown on both sides. This will take about 10 minutes.

Serve very hot.

Approximately $\frac{1}{2}$ oz. of oatmeal and a $\frac{1}{4}$ oz. dripping will be needed for each medium-sized fish.

(b) *Split and Boned*

Slit and clean the fish, place on a board, backbone upwards, and press with the thumbs along the bone to loosen it from the flesh. Turn the fish over and, beginning at the tail, prize the backbone upwards, using the thumb and forefinger. Draw the side bones away at the same time.

Work firmly and smoothly to prevent the side bones breaking off.

Dry the fish and toss in seasoned oatmeal and fry in dripping for 3–4 minutes on both sides.

Serve with *Mustard Sauce*.

½ oz. flour	2 teasp. dry mustard
½ oz. butter or margarine	1 teasp. vinegar
½ pt. milk	Salt and pepper to taste

Make the white sauce in the usual way. Blend the vinegar and mustard and add to the sauce. Reheat and test the flavour, adding more vinegar if necessary. Sometimes a pinch of sugar improves the flavour if there is a raw taste from the vinegar.

The sauce may be made with water instead of milk. In this case, increase the fat to ¾ oz.

PICKLED, POTTED OR SOUSED HERRINGS

Clean, split and bone the herrings. Replace any soft roes.

Season and roll up from head to tail, skin side outside.

Pack into a pie dish and pour round a mixture of equal quantities of vinegar and water and add spices.

Four herrings require ¼ pint water, ¼ pint vinegar, 1 blade mace, 10–12 black peppercorns, 4 cloves or 1 bay leaf, ¼ teaspoon salt.

Cover the dish and bake in a moderate oven (350° F.) for 45 minutes.

POTTED ROE

¼ *lb. cooked smoked cod's roe*	*salt, pepper to taste*
1 *shallot finely chopped*	1 *level teasp. dry mustard*
1 *oz. butter*	2 *teasp. vinegar or lemon juice*
tomato juice if liked	

Scrape the roe from the skin, add the shallot cooked till tender in the butter. Mix the mustard and vinegar or lemon juice and add with the other seasonings to the roe. Pound or put in a blender until smooth and creamy. Taste and adjust the seasoning. Pack into little pots and, if it is to be kept, cover with melted butter to seal. Serve with hot toast.

SALMON STEAKS

These may be baked or grilled and should be approximately ¾″ thick and cut from the part of the fish which will provide steaks of 4–6 oz. each.

To Bake: Wrap each steak separately in well-oiled or buttered foil. Wrap loosely but twist the open ends carefully to prevent the juices from escaping.

Cook on a baking-tray in the centre of an oven at 325° F. (moderate heat) for 20 minutes.

If to be served hot, slide from the opened foil on to a hot dish with the juices and serve with lemon and chopped parsley or hollandaise sauce.

If to be served cold, do not open the foil until the fish is quite cold.

To Grill: For each steak allow 1 teaspoon olive oil seasoned with salt and black pepper and a dash of paprika if liked. Either brush this mixture over both sides of the steaks or allow the steaks to stand in the mixture for 40 minutes, turning them over after 20 minutes.

Then grill for 10 minutes on each side under a moderate grill.

The steaks should be very lightly browned and just cooked through. Test by easing the flesh from the centre bone to see if cooked.

Serve with parsley butter, anchovy butter, hollandaise or mousseline sauce.

TROUT, SEA OR SALMON

This fish is generally cooked whole. It is smaller than a salmon and longer and narrower in shape. The flesh is less firm and more delicate in flavour and colour.

Lay the cleaned fish in a shallow pan, cover with warm 'court bouillon'. Bring slowly to boiling point. Keep near the heat so that the water is just moving for 5–10 minutes, according to size. Remove from the heat and allow to cool in the liquor. Drain when quite cold and serve as for salmon.

Court bouillon

To 1½ pints of water add 1 tbs. lemon juice, 1 teasp. salt, ½ bay leaf, 1 sprig parsley, small piece blade mace, 6 peppercorns, ½ onion, ½ carrot, 2 tbs. vinegar, tarragon for preference, 2 tbs. white wine if liked.

Bring to the boil, simmer for 20 minutes, strain and use warm.

Large cuts of Salmon: Wrap the piece of fish in greaseproof paper and cook as above allowing 10 minutes per lb. of fish and 10 minutes extra.

TROUT—LOCH OR BURN TROUT

These must be cooked while very fresh. The true flavour is obtained only when the fish is cooked and served within 2 hours of being taken from the river.

They may be grilled, poached or fried in oatmeal.

To Grill: After cleaning, slit thrice diagonally, brush with melted butter and cook for 10 minutes under a moderate grill. Serve with melted butter, flavoured with lemon juice and chopped parsley, salt and pepper.

To Poach: Lay the cleaned fish (with head on) in a shallow pan. Sprinkle with hot vinegar, cover with warm court bouillon. Bring to the boil and simmer for 10 minutes—longer if the fish is large. The fish will curl during cooking. Serve on a napkin with potatoes steamed in their jackets.

To fry in oatmeal—See herrings in oatmeal.

DRESSED CRAB

1 *medium-sized crab, boiled*	$\frac{1}{8}$ *teasp. pepper*
2 *tbs. fresh white breadcrumbs*	1 *or 2 tbs. salad oil*
1 *tbs. vinegar*	(*or cream if preferred*)
garnish	$\frac{1}{2}$ *teasp. salt*
1 *hard-boiled egg and finely chopped parsley*	

Rinse the crab under running water.

Remove the claws, crack the shells and remove the white meat. Use the point of a skewer if necessary to remove the flesh from the tips of the small claws.

Separate the body from the shell; remove and burn the bag near the mouth and the small feathery gills, as some of these are poisonous.

Remove any creamy meat from inside the shell and the body of the crab, using a teaspoon. Chop the meat well and mix it with the meat from the claws.

Add the breadcrumbs to the chopped crab meat; add the vinegar, oil and seasonings.

Scrub the shell thoroughly, dry it; break round the natural line by pressing with the thumbs and polish it with a very little olive oil.

Fill the shell with the prepared crab mixture.

Chop the egg white very finely, sieve the egg yolk; chop the parsley very finely.

Decorate the crab by arranging the egg white, egg yolk and chopped parsley in sections.

Finally, garnish with the small claws previously washed, dried and trimmed.

PARTAN PIE (*Crab Pie*)
(Based on Meg Dod's Recipe)

Remove the meat from the shell and claws of a medium-sized crab. Scrub the shell. Mix the crab meat with salt, pepper and nutmeg to taste.

Add 2 tbs. fine white breadcrumbs and 1 oz. unsalted butter.

Add 3 or 4 tbs. vinegar and 1 teasp. made mustard.

Stir over a moderate heat until thoroughly hot.

Return to the shell and place under a grill heated to maximum until brown. Serve at once.

TO PREPARE A LOBSTER

All the meat of a lobster is edible with the exception of the spinal cord, a thin black vein which runs through the middle of the underside of the tail meat, and the stomach which is a hard sack or bag in the right side of the head.

1. Twist off the claws, keep the small ones for garnish.

2. Lay the lobster on its back and cut lengthways from head to tail along the division of the shell. Use a pair of scissors or a sharp knife.

3. Remove the cord in the tail and the bag in the head and discard. Remove the coral, wash and lay aside for decoration or for flavouring sauce or butter.

4. Take care not to break the antennae as the head shell forms the focal point of the decoration of a lobster dish.

5. Remove the meat from the shell of the body and tail. Crack the pincer claws with a hammer or nutcracker and pick out the meat. Keep the pieces as large as possible. Include the green meat or liver as this is one of the choicest parts.

LOBSTER SALAD

Polish the shell and antennae with a little oil. Pack the lobster flesh back into the shells and arrange shining side uppermost on a bed of lettuce and watercress. Stand the head in a 'rearing' position and decorate the dish with the small claws and the black pincer ends of the large claws. Garnish with cucumber and, if liked, tomato and hard-boiled egg. Serve with mayonnaise dressing.

Meat and Game Dishes

MEAT AND GAME DISHES

For many generations Scotland has produced prime beef and small mountain mutton and lamb which are of superb quality and flavour. Much of the superlative quality meat is sent to England and, in fact, the 'Roast Beef of Old England', at its best has, for generations, been Scottish in origin. The demand for grilling cuts has increased considerably since the Second World War and the introduction of Steak Houses has helped towards the growing popularity of choice cuts of Scots beef.

Many of the recipes show some development from the stewpot, and dishes like haggis show the skill of the frugal Scots housewife in making a delicious and nourishing dish out of humble ingredients. Though she, like other women, now buys more of the expensive cuts of meat which are more quickly cooked, the Scots housewife serves dishes made from the cheaper cuts more frequently than her English counterpart.

The Scots have always tended to eat more fish than meat, but there are many traditional dishes of beef and mutton which make particularly good eating. Pork is not popular in most parts, being especially unpopular in the Highlands, due to prejudice. In the lowland countries there are old recipes using pickled pork.

The hills and moors are still a source of grouse, partridge, pheasant, hares and rabbits, and the traditional recipes use both young and old game. The amount of game in the shops indicates the inclusion of game in the ordinary family's meals. Venison is available throughout the season which lasts from June to December. Venison is sold as game and is ready hung when bought. It is a very close meat, satisfying and rather strong in flavour. It is economical to buy, being cheaper than beef and served in smaller portions. Many people consider it an acquired taste.

BEEF BALLS

1 *lb. minced shoulder steak*
6 *oz. suet minced with the beef*
½ *teasp. freshly ground black pepper*

1 *teasp. salt*
¼ *teasp. each of ground cloves, ginger and mace*
1 *beaten egg to mix*

The flavouring of these balls is very much a matter of taste and many people like a different proportion of ground spices. Sugar is often added and the dark, moist brown sugar is particularly successful.

Mix all the ingredients together and taste carefully.

Roll into balls of a size suitable for portioning.

Roll in medium oatmeal or breadcrumbs.

Fry a rich brown colour. It is easier to do this in deep fat, and the beef balls, being uncooked, require a temperature of 350°–360° F. for 5–7 minutes, according to size.

When using frying oil, it is important to check the temperature as the hazing point varies according to the type of oil and many do not haze until the temperature of the oil is too hot for frying.

FORFAR BRIDIES

1 *lb. topside or shoulder steak*
3 *oz. shredded suet*
2 *tbs. onion finely chopped*

salt and freshly ground pepper to taste
1 *lb. paste to cover*

Traditionally the paste is made of flour, salt and water only, but as the raw meat is put into the paste, it is difficult to produce a finished bridie which is not hard and tough on the outside.

Many Scots housewives make a good shortcrust or a suet pastry, but these too are often hard if baked long enough to allow the meat to cook.

A rough puff or flaky pastry will withstand the time and temperature required to cook the meat thoroughly and is therefore to be recommended.

Beat the topside well with a rolling pin and cut into thin strips. If the cheaper cut of meat is used, mince it. Mix with onion and seasoning.

Roll the pastry into 3 or 4 rounds or ovals. Cover half of each piece of paste with the meat. Damp the edges of the paste and fold the spare paste over the meat to produce a half moon shape. Press the edges together and crimp as desired. Make a hole in the top to allow steam to escape.

Bake at 400° F. for 20 minutes if short pastry or 425° F. for 20 minutes if flaky or rough puff. Reduce the heat to 350° F. and continue cooking until the meat is tender, about another hour. Serve hot.

FOWL BOILED WITH OATMEAL STUFFING

One fowl trussed for boiling, i.e. with the legs pushed up next the breast under the loosened skin and the skin drawn smoothly over the breast and legs.

To cook with the fowl:

1 *onion*
1 *carrot*
1 *celery stick or*
½ *teasp. celery seed*
2 *cloves*
slices of lemon

blade of mace
1 *bay leaf*
6 *black peppercorns*
1 *teasp. salt to each*
1 *lb. of bird weight*

43

Stuffing

4 oz. medium oatmeal

2 oz. shredded suet or
grated cooking fat

2 tbs. finely chopped onion

pepper and salt

Parboil the onion and chop. Mix with the meal and suet and add enough seasoning to give a good flavour. This is important as too little salt will mean a flat taste and too much will make the whole bird salty.

Pack some of the stuffing into the neck end of the bird and the remainder into the body and then sew up the opening at the tail end. Use the pope's nose to help to keep the flesh secure. The cavity must not be tightly packed as the stuffing will swell on cooking and will burst open the stitching if there is too much stuffing or the stitching is not secure.

Cooking the Fowl

Rub the breast with the slices of lemon. If the flavour of lemon is much liked, lay slices on the breast before wrapping the bird in greaseproof paper or buttermuslin (or an old linen tea towel).

Put the bird into a roomy pan and cover with cold water. Add the prepared vegetables and flavourings. Bring slowly to simmering point and cook slowly for $1\frac{1}{4}$–3 hours according to the age of the bird. When the drumstick is tender the bird is cooked.

Remove the bird from the liquor. Drain well and remove the paper or cloth and thread.

If to be eaten hot, serve with the vegetables from the pot, mashed together, and boiled potatoes.

A sauce made from $\frac{1}{2}$ liquor and $\frac{1}{2}$ milk, to which chopped hard-boiled egg and parsley are added, makes an excellent addition.

If the bird is to be served cold, allow it to cool in the liquor, drain and dry well and coat with the sauce. The flavour of the oatmeal stuffing permeates the whole bird and makes a gourmet's dish of the humble boiled fowl.

GAME

Game birds each have their own season and at other times may not (by law) be shot or sold. The season for game, generally speaking, is from August to February. With the introduction of deep freezing, it is possible sometimes to buy deep frozen game out of season but this is not a common practice.

The young game birds are suitable for roasting but even so they must be hung for a while in order that the flesh shall be tender and have flavour. In England it is customary to serve roast game slightly underdone after quick roasting but most Scottish families prefer birds, like meat, cooked through. They must be hung by the neck, unplucked and undrawn, in a cool larder or outhouse until the tail feathers pull out easily. This will take from 5–12 days according to age and the type of bird and the taste of those who will eat it. The longer the bird has hung the more pronounced will be the 'gamey' or 'high' flavour.

After hanging, the birds are plucked, drawn and trussed like a chicken but the feet are left on. This is because the feet of the old birds are hard and scaly and the claws long—thus the age of the bird is indicated. Before the cooked bird comes to table the claws can be trimmed if necessary. Birds bought at the poulterers are ready trussed and the claws cut off.

ROAST GAME

Grouse: In season 12th Aug.–10th Dec. Average cooking time 45 minutes.

Partridge: In season 1st Sept.–1st Feb. Average cooking time 30 minutes.

Pheasant: In season 1st Oct.–1st Feb. Average cooking time 45–60 minutes.

These are the most plentiful birds in Scotland.

Game birds tend to be dry, so cover the breast with fat bacon and put a nut of seasoned butter in the body cavity. Some people like a piece of raw steak put inside as well. Put the bird into hot fat, butter for preference, baste well and cook at 375° F. for 30–60 minutes according to the size of the bird. Baste during cooking or cook wrapped in greased paper. Ten minutes before the bird is done, remove the paper and fat bacon, dredge the breast with flour, baste well and return to the oven to brown. Serve with clear gravy, bread sauce, fried crumbs, game chips, a green salad and watercress to garnish. Cranberry sauce is an accompaniment which is often served.

To make clear gravy: Remove the bird on to a hot ashet, take out any trussing strings and keep the bird hot. Pour off any fat in the tin, leaving the sediment. Sprinkle with flour to absorb any trace of fat. Mix well and season. Brown if necessary. Add stock made from the giblets of the bird, boil up, taste and serve. It should be well flavoured, a good brown colour and thin in consistency.

GAME CASSEROLED

Old birds are difficult to make tender unless cooked in liquid. They may be stewed or braised in the same way as meat and the mixture of vegetables can include mushrooms and tomatoes, either fresh or tinned, or tomato paste. If a bouillon cube is used to produce stock, use a beef cube rather than a chicken cube.

Both grouse and pheasant need 1½–2½ hours very slow cooking. To produce a dish of superb quality from old birds, soak in a marinade for several hours, overnight if possible.

The following is suitable for any game:

¼ *pint red wine*
2 *tbs. salad oil*
2 *sliced shallots*
slice of lemon or orange peel if liked

4–6 *black peppercorns*
sprig of fresh thyme and marjoram
2 *bay leaves*

Put all together in a pan and bring to the boil. Cool. Meanwhile, cut the backs of the birds away with scissors and remove the feet. Put the birds in a casserole and pour over the cold marinade. Leave 6–24 hours, turning the meat once or twice if it is not covered. After soaking, remove the backs and stew for stock. Add enough stock to the birds in the marinade to ensure the meat is covered. Simmer in the covered casserole until tender 1½–2½ hours according to the age of the bird. Thicken with beurre manié, test the seasoning and serve with potatoes baked in their skins, a green salad and rowan jelly.

This recipe is very suitable for pigeons.

Beurre Manié, or kneaded butter, is made by working equal quantities of butter and flour together until they form a smooth paste. Pieces about the size of a hazelnut are added one by one to the liquid, which should be at simmering point. Shake the pan, or whisk with a fork so that the liaison and the liquid are well blended and a smooth consistency is obtained.

HAGGIS

The traditional Haggis is prepared from the sheep's pluck (liver, lights and heart) and is cooked in the stomach bag. This bag needs a great deal of preparation before it can be used and many people find the cleaning and scraping of the bag very distasteful. The quantity of haggis prepared from a pluck is often more than is required by a household even though the cooked dish will keep for several days in a refrigerator, or cool larder.

The following recipe gives a savoury dish of excellent food value and is easy to prepare. It is known as 'Pot Haggis' or 'Pan Haggis'.

½ lb. liver or
¼ lb. liver and a sheep's heart
1 onion (¼ lb. approx.)
2 oz. beef suet

salt and pepper
3 oz. pinhead oatmeal
liquor from the liver (approx. ½ pint)

Wash the liver and heart thoroughly and cook with the onions for 30–40 minutes until tender. When cool mince the meat and chop the onion.

Put the oatmeal in a heavy frying-pan and stir over heat until lightly brown.

If the suet has been bought in a piece, shred on a coarse grater.

Mix with the liver, onion, seasonings, oatmeal and enough liquor from the liver to make a soft dropping consistency. The pepper should be freshly milled black pepper.

Steam for 2 hours in a greased basin covered with foil to prevent condensed steam dropping into the mixture.

Serve with mashed turnip (neeps) and potatoes.

When a traditionally made haggis is served at a Burns Supper, it is piped in with great ceremony and in addition to neeps and tatties, nips of whisky are offered.

HARE

In Scotland, only the very choice fillets from the back of the hare are served as a main dish, the rest being used for soup. Most recipes assume that the hare will be freshly killed and must be skinned and cleaned and therefore the blood can be collected in a cup. Sometimes in country areas, the fishmonger will retain the blood so that a customer can collect the hare blood in a basin, but most people prefer to prepare the dish without the blood, having bought the hare ready skinned and cleaned. If it is intended to remove the fillets of choice meat from the back of the hare, the fishmonger must be asked to send the animal whole.

HARE SOUP

1 *hare cut up after removing the back fillets*	2 *bay leaves*
2 *oz. dripping*	1 *bouquet garni*
2 *onions*	½ *teasp. peppercorns*
2 *carrots*	2–3 *teasp. salt*
2 *sticks celery*	1 *glass port*
3 *oz. medium oatmeal*	*red currant jelly*

Cover the hare with cold water. Bring to the boil. Pour off the water. Dry the joints and fry in the dripping till brown. Drain. Put into a clean pan and cover again with cold water. Add the cut up vegetables and seasonings. Simmer for 3 hours. Strain the liquor, add the oatmeal and cook for 15 minutes. Add the port wine and redcurrant jelly and chopped meat from the legs to make a thick soup which, when served with boiled potatoes, makes a very satisfying main course in a meal.

JUGGED HARE

Take the fillets from the back of a hare. Toss in seasoned flour and fry in hot dripping (1 oz.) until brown all over. Remove. Pieces of fat bacon may be fried to provide fat for this. Add chopped onion to the fat and fry till brown, add enough flour to absorb any surplus fat. Make into a thin brown sauce with liquor from the hare soup. Add a bouquet garni, a small bay leaf, a clove and a few peppercorns. Bring to the boil and skim. Add salt to taste. Put the pieces of hare in a casserole,

49

cover with the liquid and cook in a slow oven until the meat is tender. This will probably take 2–2½ hours at least.

If possible, allow to stand overnight to mellow. Re-heat thoroughly.

Just before serving, remove the herbs and spices, add a glass of port and enough redcurrant jelly to give a good flavour. Serve with forcemeat balls.

The liver may be pounded and added to the gravy with the wine and jelly.

MINCE COLLOPS

1 *lb. steak minced with about 1 oz. suet (topside or shoulder steak)*
2 *small onions chopped*

1 *teasp. salt*
pepper to taste
½–¾ *pint stock*
1 *tbs. oatmeal*

Put the minced steak into a heavy pan and heat while separating the grains of meat, until the meat is beginning to brown. Stir in the oatmeal and seasoning and then add enough stock almost to cover the meat. Simmer for ¾–1 hour.

Serve with toast or mashed potatoes.

To vary the flavour, mushroom ketchup or Worcester Sauce may be added during the cooking. Breadcrumbs may be substituted for oatmeal; the oatmeal may be toasted before adding to the mince.

Some people cook the onion whole in with the meat and remove before serving.

The collop may be served on toast topped by a poached egg. Minced hare or venison may be used instead of beef.

MUTTON PIES

Filling

½ *lb. lean mutton*
1 *shallot chopped finely*
½ *teasp. chopped parsley and thyme (mixed)*

2 *chopped mushrooms if liked*
2 *tbs. good stock*
1–2 *teasp. mushroom ketchup*
salt and pepper

Pastry

¾ lb. flour   ½ teasp. salt
3 oz. dripping or lard   1½ gills water

Chop the meat small, rejecting any skin or gristle. Mix with
the flavourings.

Sieve the flour and salt into a bowl. Boil the water and as
soon as the dripping has melted, pour into the flour and mix
well, using a wooden spoon until the mixture is cool enough
to handle. Knead until smooth.

Cut off about ¼ of the paste and keep warm and covered.
Divide the remainder into 4, roll out lightly and line 4 pie
rings (large pastry cutters will suffice).

Fill with the meat mixture and add ½ tbs. stock to each
pie. Damp the edges of the pastry and cover each pie with a
lid made from ¼ of the remaining pastry. Press the edges of
the paste together, trim and crimp.

Make a hole in the centre of each top, and brush the lid
with egg or milk.

Bake at 375° F. for 40 minutes. Remove the rings after
30 minutes and, if necessary, cover the pies with paper to
prevent further browning. Fill up the pie with hot stock if
necessary. Serve at once.

POTTED HEID OR HOUGH

½ ox cheek or 1 lb. shin of beef (hough)
1 ox foot or pig's trotter
small blade of mace, 2 allspice and a bouquet garni
2 teasp. salt, 2 cloves and pepper to taste

Wash the foot and scrape away fat and marrow. Scald the
cheek and the foot. If shin is used, cut up. Put the foot,
broken into pieces, and the cheek or pieces of shin into a pan.
Cover with cold water, add the salt, allspice, freshly ground

pepper or peppercorns, a blade of mace, bouquet garni and 2 cloves.

Cook very slowly until the meat falls from the bones, probably about 3 hours. Strain off the meat and bones, retain the liquor. Cut the meat coarsely, removing the spices and any skin and bones. Return the liquor to the pan and reduce. The liquor will contain gelatine from the foot and will help the setting. Test the flavour. Strain over the meat which has been put into wetted moulds and allow to set.

RABBIT PIE OR KINGDOM OF FIFE PIE

2 *small rabbits*	*grated nutmeg, salt, pepper*
¾ *lb. pickled pork*	1 *oz. dripping*
2 *hard-boiled eggs*	

12 oz. flour made into rough puff pastry.

Cut up the skinned and cleaned rabbits. Make a good stock from the forelegs, ribs and head. Fry the joints of rabbit in the dripping, drain and place in a pie-dish. Add the pickled pork and seasonings. Cut the eggs into quarters and arrange in the dish.

Add, if liked, forcemeat made from:

pounded rabbit livers	*salt and pepper*
3 *oz. breadcrumbs*	1 *teasp. chopped parsley*
1 *oz. chopped bacon*	*a little thyme and marjoram*
egg to bind	

Pour in enough stock to come two-thirds up the pie-dish. Cover with pastry. Make two or three slits in the pie crust. Put into the oven at 425° F. for 15 minutes and then reduce the heat to 325° F. and cook for a further 1½–2 hours. Cover with paper if the pastry becomes too brown. Brush with egg to glaze about 10 minutes before serving. If necessary, fill up the pie-dish with well flavoured boiling hot stock before serving.

SHEEP'S HEAD PIE

1 *sheep's head*   1 *level teasp. salt*
4 *sheep's trotters*   6 *black peppercorns*
2 *hard-boiled eggs*   *water to cover*

Remove the brains from the head and wash in cold water to which ½ teasp. vinegar has been added. Soak the head and trotters for 24 hours, changing the water at least once during this process. Rinse the head and make sure all the clots of blood are removed. Rub over the head and trotters with the brains. Put the head and trotters into a pan with water to which salt is added and bring slowly to the boil. Add the peppercorns and simmer 2–3 hours till the flesh is coming away from the bones. Remove from the liquid and slice the flesh thinly. Skin the tongue and slice thinly. Into a pie-dish place half of the meat. Arrange the hard-boiled eggs, either cut in half or sliced on the layer of meat and cover with the rest of the meat. Reduce the stock and pour over the meat. Serve cold with salad.

STUFFED SKIRTING STEAK

1 *lb. skirting steak*   1 *onion, peeled and sliced*
1 *oz. dripping*   *carrot and turnip*
1 *oz. flour*   1 *level teasp. salt*
1 *pint stock or water*   *pepper*

Stuffing

4 *oz. medium oatmeal*   1 *small onion*
2 *oz. suet*   *salt, pepper*
1 *tbs. chopped parsley*   *milk or water*

Ask the butcher to leave the steak in one piece. Remove the skin from one side only. Loosen the skin on the second side to form a 'pocket'. Mix together all the ingredients for the stuffing and put into the prepared 'pocket'. Sew together with coarse thread or very fine string.

Melt the dripping in a stew pan and, when hot, brown the meat on both sides and the onion. Add the stock and seasoning, bring to the boil and simmer slowly 2½ hours. Approximately an hour before serving add blocks of carrot and turnip, and 20 minutes before serving, thicken the gravy with blended flour. Place the meat on a hot ashet and remove the thread before straining over the gravy and garnishing with the blocks of carrot and turnip.

VENISON PATTIES

8 oz. flaky pastry

Filling

4 oz. cooked venison   1 gill cranberry sauce

Although this has been made for many years, the recipe can be brought up to date by using prepared pastry.

Dice the venison from the remains of a roast or a braise and moisten well with the cranberry sauce. Line flat patty tins with rounds of pastry and put in the filling. Damp the edges and cover with a round of pastry. Knock up and flute the edges and make a hole in the top. Bake 15–20 minutes in an oven heated to 420° F. then reduce the heat to 375° F. Bake 40–45 minutes altogether till the pastry is cooked to the centre and the filling thoroughly hot.

Serve hot or cold.

As an alternative filling, cook 2 oz. soaked prunes in ½ gill port wine.

Cut up the prunes, add to 4 oz. diced cooked venison and 1 gill of rich brown sauce, to which the surplus port wine has been added.

VENISON AND PIGEON PIE

2 *pigeons*	*black pepper*
½ *lb. stewing venison*	*pinch of nutmeg*
1 *tbs. flour*	*good beef stock*
½ *teasp. salt*	½ *lb. flaky or rough puff pastry*

Use only the breasts filleted from the pigeons and discard the rest of the birds. Slice the meat thinly. Toss in the flour, salt, pepper and nutmeg. Pack the venison and pigeons in layers in a pie-dish. Half fill the dish with stock. Cover with flaky pastry in the usual way. Make a cross cut in the centre of the crust and decorate round this cut with leaves of pastry cut from the trimmings.

Cook in the middle of the oven at 425° F. (No. 7 Gas) until the pastry is well risen and set, then reduce to 325° F. (No. 3 Gas) and continue cooking till the meat is tender, 1½–2 hours in all. When the pastry is a good brown colour, cover the pie with greaseproof paper to prevent burning.

VENISON BRAISED

Braise

1½–2 *lbs. haunch of venison*	½ *pint stock*
1 *oz. dripping*	1 *orange*
1 *onion*	1 *tbs. redcurrant or cranberry jelly*
1 *carrot* (*medium*)	1 *teasp. salt*
4 *sticks celery*	

Marinade

2 *glasses red wine*	4 *large black peppercorns*
1 *tbs. oil*	6 *allspice or juniper berries*
1 *sliced onion*	*parsley stalks*
1 *bay leaf*	1 *oz. kneaded butter* (*see casseroled game*) *to thicken*

Heat the ingredients of the marinade to boiling point. Cool. Tie the meat into shape, put into a deep dish. Pour the cool marinade over the meat. Leave 24–48 hours, turning once or twice if necessary. Drain and dry. Melt the dripping in a fireproof casserole and brown the meat on all sides. Remove from the casserole and put the prepared braise vegetables with strips of orange peel into the dripping. Cover the casserole and cook slowly for 5–10 minutes until the onion is soft. Be careful not to burn the vegetables. Add the herbs, spices, the strained liquid from the marinade and the stock. Lay the joint of meat on the bed of vegetables and cook slowly very tightly covered either in the oven or on the top of the stove for $1\frac{1}{2}$–$2\frac{1}{2}$ hours, until the venison is tender.

To dish: Put the meat on a deep dish. Keep hot. Strain the stock from the braise vegetables, pick out the herbs and serve the vegetables with the meat. Put the liquor into the casserole, add the orange juice and jelly to flavour. Thicken with the kneaded butter, test the flavour and serve round the joint or in a sauceboat.

VENISON STEWED OR CIVET OF VENISON

$1\frac{1}{2}$ *lb. stewing venison cut into pieces suitable for serving*
2 oz. belly pork cut into $\frac{1}{2}''$ cubes
1 teasp. minced parsley
2 medium onions (about $\frac{1}{2}$ lb.)
1 crushed clove of garlic if liked
2 oz. mushrooms
1 tbs. wine vinegar

1 glass red wine
enough stock just to cover the meat
1 teasp. salt
3 or 4 black peppercorns
1 oz. flour
a little butter or dripping to start the fat of the pork running

Melt the butter in a flameproof casserole, add the cubes of pork fat and cook until the fat runs out. Fry the pieces of venison in the dripping till brown and remove. Run off excess dripping, leaving 1 tbs. Mix in the flour and make a brown roux. Add the flamed wine, vinegar and stock, bring to the boil, skim and season. Add the parsley, onions, garlic and meat. Cook slowly, tightly covered for 2–2½ hours until the venison is tender. Do not overcook. Add sliced mushrooms, half an hour before serving, when the meat is almost tender. Serve in the casserole.

A hare or rabbit may be cooked in this way and both make an excellent civet.

Meatless Dishes

MEATLESS DISHES

OATMEAL PUDDING

8 oz. medium oatmeal
4 oz. suet
2 small onions
2 level teasp. salt

1 large pinch of bicarbonate of
soda
cold water

Mix together the oatmeal, suet, salt and bicarbonate of soda.
Chop the onions very finely or grate and add to the oatmeal.
Add sufficient cold water to form a soft dropping consistency
when mixed. Pour into a greased basin, cover with greased
paper or foil and steam 1½–1¾ hours. Turn out and serve with
a brown or tomato sauce.

Grilled bacon rolls may be served with the oatmeal
pudding.

SKIRLIE

4 oz. medium oatmeal
2 oz. dripping

1 onion
salt, pepper

Melt the dripping in a thick frying-pan. Chop the onion
finely and fry very slowly in the dripping till soft. Add the
oatmeal and fry slowly, stirring from time to time till the

oatmeal is well cooked, crisp and light brown. Season thoroughly and serve very hot with mashed potato and mashed turnip or cooked cabbage.

STOVIES

1 *lb. potatoes*   ½ *oz. dripping*
¼ *lb. onions*   1 *gill water*
salt, pepper

Prepare the vegetables, slicing the potatoes thickly and the onions thinly. Melt the dripping in a pan with a strong, thick base and fry the onion slices lightly. Add the potatoes, season well and pour over the water. Bring to the boil and simmer gently for approximately 1 hour. Stir occasionally to prevent the vegetables from sticking. Serve very hot.

Small quantities of meat, poultry, game left from a previous meal, cut in dice and added 10–15 minutes before serving, add flavour and a small amount of nutritive value to the dish.

Stovies may be cooked very successfully for a longer period of time in a casserole in the simmering oven of a heat storage cooker or in the slow heat of a gas or electric oven.

Baking

BAKING

When peat was the only fuel in use in Scotland, every home possessed a bakestone on which the women of the family cooked the bannocks which played an important part in the normal diet. The bannocks were made daily from home-grown barley and oats ground locally. They were unleavened, rather like the present-day oatcakes, and until the introduction of chemical raising agents in the nineteenth century, the ordinary housewife did not vary the bannocks much. When the girdle superseded the bakestone, the firing of the bannocks was much easier for the housewife.

In the more populated areas where some people could afford to buy the products of the baxters or bakers, the tea breads and cakes were known as long as four or five centuries ago. These owe much to the French, who came over during the period of the Auld Alliance, but could be afforded regularly only by those who could pay for goods made from expensive wheat flour and dried fruit, both of which had to be imported. The baxters or bakers used yeast as a leavening agent, but until the cost of wheaten flour came within the economic possibility of the ordinary housewife, these loaves and cakes were not much made at home. Now they are made in many homes and are still a great attraction to visitors to this country where tea is the most famous of the meals.

The industrial section of the agricultural shows are very popular and the sections which deal with home baking are well supported, thus proving that housewives still practise the traditional skills, even though the baker's van now visits even the most remote areas regularly. A good home baker has great prestige among her circle of friends, and mothers do their best to hand on their skills to their daughters. Modern ingredients are reliable and such commodities as self-raising flour, high-grade easily used fats and pre-packed washed fruit take any drudgery out of the art and craft of baking.

AYRSHIRE SHORTBREAD

7 oz. flour	2 oz. castor sugar
1 oz. cornflour	¼ egg
4 oz. butter	½ teasp. cream

Sieve together the flour and cornflour and cream the butter and sugar lightly. Add the egg and cream and, using the hand, work in the flour. When of a firm consistency and smooth, place on a floured working surface and roll into an oblong not less than ¼" in thickness. Prick all over and cut into fingers 4" × 1½". Lay on a tray covered with a sheet of paper and bake 15–20 minutes in an oven heated to 300° F. (No. 2 in a gas oven). When cooked and very lightly coloured, dredge with castor sugar and cool on a wire tray.

If preferred, make into a round cake, prick round the edge to decorate and bake 40–45 minutes.

BAPS

½ lb. flour	½ oz. yeast
1 level teasp. salt	4 tbs. milk
1 oz. cooking fat or lard	4 tbs. water

Sieve the flour and salt into a warm bowl and work in the fat. Crumble the yeast into the warm milk and water and add to the flour. Beat the mixture till smooth using the hand. Place the bowl in a polythene bag and leave in a warm place till the dough has doubled its size. Turn out on to a floured working surface and knead thoroughly. Divide into 6 and shape into flat oval rolls. Place on a greased tray, cover with the polythene bag and place in a warm place for 15 minutes. Brush with milk and bake in an oven heated to 430° F. for approximately 15 minutes. Serve hot or cold for breakfast.

If floury baps are preferred, dust with flour before putting into the oven.

BLACK BUN

Paste

6 *oz. flour*	2 *oz. mixed fats*
½ *level teasp. salt*	1½ *tbs. water*
½ *level teasp. baking powder*	

Filling

5 *oz. flour*	1 *level teasp. ground cinnamon*
½ *level teasp. bicarbonate of soda*	10 *oz. raisins*
¾ *level teasp. cream of tartar*	10 *oz. currants*
3 *oz. moist sugar*	2 *oz. almonds*
½ *level teasp. black pepper*	1 *oz. mixed peel*
1 *level teasp. Jamaica pepper*	4 *tbs. milk*
1 *level teasp. ground ginger*	1 *teasp. brandy*

To make the paste sieve the flour, salt and baking powder and work in the fat. Mix to a stiff paste with water. On a lightly floured working surface divide into two-thirds and one-third. Knead each piece till smooth. Roll out the larger piece to a circle to fit the base and sides of a round 5″ cake-tin. Line the tin, being careful to avoid pleats of paste on the sides. A tin with a loose base is the most convenient to use.

To make the filling sieve the flour, raising agents and spices. Add the sugar and the fruit, prepared according to kind, i.e.

wash and dry the raisins and currants and chop the almonds after removing the brown skin. Stir in the milk and brandy and, when all is thoroughly mixed, put into the lined tin. Press down and leave at least $\frac{1}{2}''$ of paste above the filling.

To finish roll out the rest of the paste to a circle large enough to cover the filling. Wet the edges of the lining and top and press together. Brush the top with beaten egg and pierce the lid and filling several times with a skewer. Prick over the top. Bake in the middle of an oven heated to 350° F. (No. 4 in a gas oven) for approximately 2 hours. Turn out and cool on a wire tray and store in a covered tin for several weeks before using, in order to mellow.

BORDER TART

Pastry

4 oz. flour
pinch salt
$\frac{3}{8}$ oz. yeast
$1\frac{1}{2}$ oz. mixed fat
$\frac{1}{2}$ gill milk

Filling

4 oz. almond paste
1 oz. chopped almonds
1 oz. sultanas
1 oz. peel

Confectioner's Custard

$\frac{3}{4}$ oz. cornflour
1 oz. butter
$\frac{3}{4}$ gill milk
$\frac{1}{2}$ egg
2 level teasp. castor sugar
2 drops vanilla essence

Glacé Icing

1 oz. icing sugar
warm water

To make the pastry sieve together the flour and salt. Crumble the yeast into the warm milk and add to the flour. Beat all together with the hand till smooth and elastic. Put the bowl in a polythene bag and leave to rise to double its size in about 45 minutes. Cool and then roll out to a long strip. Add the mixed fats in small pieces over two-thirds of the paste, fold as for flaky pastry and half turn. Roll into a circle and line a lightly greased 7" sandwich tin. Trim the edges.

Filling: roll the almond paste to a 6½" circle and place on the pastry. Sprinkle on the almonds, sultanas and peel. Make a sauce with the cornflour, margarine and milk. Cool and add the sugar, egg and flavouring. Mix well. Pour over the fruit.

Roll out the trimmings of pastry and cut 5 circles 1" in diameter. Lay these on the confectioner's custard. Cover with a piece of greased paper and prove in a warm place for 15 minutes.

Bake 35–40 minutes in an oven heated to 400° F. (No. 6 in a gas oven). After 20 minutes reduce the heat to 375° F. When cooked, remove from the tin and cool on a wire tray. When cold, ice the pastry circles with glacé icing, made by mixing the icing sugar with enough warm water to make a coating consistency.

ALMOND PASTE

2 oz. ground almonds	½ teasp. lemon juice
2 oz. castor sugar	¼ teasp. vanilla essence
beaten egg	1–2 drops almond essence

Mix the ground almonds and sugar and add the flavourings. Use sufficient egg to bind together, turn on to a working surface dusted with icing sugar and knead lightly till smooth.

If preferred, in place of 2 oz. castor sugar use 2 oz. icing sugar or 1 oz. castor sugar and 1 oz. icing sugar.

BRANDY WAFERS

2 oz. flour	1 level teasp. ground ginger
2 oz. margarine or butter	grated rind of ½ lemon
2 oz. castor sugar	4 oz. syrup

Filling

¼ pint whipped, sweetened cream

Put the margarine, sugar and syrup into a pan and heat gently till the fat is melted. Remove from the heat and stir in the other ingredients. Grease 3 or 4 baking-trays and drop the mixture on to them, using a teaspoon. Allow 4–5″ between each teaspoonful. Bake approximately 10 minutes in an oven heated to 330° F. (No. 3 if using a gas oven). When very thin and golden brown remove from the oven and allow to stand for a short time to set slightly. Ease from the tray with a broad-bladed knife and wrap lightly round the greased handle of a wooden spoon. When set, slip off on to a wire tray. Pipe cream into either end of the wafers an hour or two before serving.

The wafers may be stored in a tin with a tight-fitting lid for a few days, without the cream.

When curling keep the smooth side of the wafer to the handle of the spoon.

BROONIE

4 oz. flour	1½ level teasp. bicarbonate of soda
4 oz. medium oatmeal	2 level teasp. ground ginger
2 oz. margarine	2 tbs. treacle
3 oz. moist sugar	1 egg
sour or buttermilk	

Heat an oven to 330° F. and grease a 6″ tin. Sieve the flour, spice and bicarbonate of soda and rub in the fat. Add the oatmeal, sugar, melted treacle and the egg. Pour in sufficient milk to make a soft consistency when mixed. Pour into the tin and bake in the centre of the oven from 1–1½ hours. When cooked, cool on a wire tray.

CRUMPETS

4 oz. flour
1 level teasp. bicarbonate of soda
2 level teasp. cream of tartar
2 tbs. castor sugar

1 teasp. melted margarine
1½ gills milk
1 large egg

Sieve together all the dry ingredients, add the margarine, egg and milk and beat till smooth. Heat a girdle slowly and when hot grease with a knob of fat in a screw of paper. Pour the mixture from the point of a large tablespoon on to the girdle. Cook on the first side till brown, turn and cook on the second side. Cool in a towel or spread with butter, roll up and serve hot.

The crumpets will be smooth and brown on one side and covered with small holes on the other side.

DATE AND WALNUT BREAD

¾ lb. self-raising flour
2 level teasp. baking powder
2 oz. castor sugar
2 oz. cooking dates

2 oz. walnuts
1 tbs. syrup
1 tbs. treacle
½ pint milk

Sieve the flour and baking powder and add the sugar. Chop the dates and walnuts and add to the flour. Warm the syrup and treacle and add to the mixture with the milk. Mix to a dropping consistency. Put into a greased 1 lb. loaf tin and bake 45–50 minutes in the middle of an oven heated to 350° F. (No. 4 in a gas oven). Remove from the tin and cool. Use the following day, sliced thinly and spread with butter.

DUNDEE CAKE

8 oz. flour
1 level teasp. baking powder
5 oz. butter
5 oz. castor sugar
2 level tbs. ground almonds
3 eggs

6 oz. currants
6 oz. sultanas
2 oz. glacé cherries
2 oz. mixed peel
grated rind of ½ lemon
split almonds

Line a round 7″ cake-tin with greased paper. Prepare the fruit; sieve the flour and baking powder. Cream the butter and sugar till light and fluffy. Beat in the eggs, one by one, adding a small quantity of flour if the mixture shows a tendency to curdle. Stir in the flour, ground almonds, fruit and lemon rind. Turn into the lined tin and make a depression in the centre. Place in the middle of an oven heated to 330° F. (No. 3 in a gas oven) and bake 2–2½ hours. After ½ hour cover the top of the cake with split almonds, rounded side uppermost.

A less expensive cake can be made by substituting all or part of the butter with margarine, but neither the flavour nor the keeping quality will be as good.

FOCHABERS GINGERBREAD

1 lb. flour
2 level teasp. bicarbonate of soda
½ lb. mixed fats
¼ lb. castor sugar
¼ lb. sultanas
¼ lb. currants
3 oz. mixed peel
3 oz. ground almonds

2 level teasp. mixed spice
4 level teasp. ground ginger
2 level teasp. ground cinnamon
1 level teasp. ground cloves
½ lb. treacle
2 eggs
½ pint beer or ale

Mix the prepared fruit together. Sieve the flour and spices. Cream the margarine and sugar and add the treacle, previously melted. Beat in the eggs, one at a time. Work in the flour, ground almonds and dried fruit. Dissolve the bicarbonate of soda in the beer and stir into the mixture. Divide between two lightly greased round 5″ cake-tins or put into one lightly greased 8″ tin. Bake in the centre of an oven heated to 300° F. for 1¾–2 hours for two cakes, 2½–3 hours for one cake. Remove from the tin and cool. Store in a tightly covered tin.

GINGER SHORTCAKE

6 *oz. self-raising flour*	4 *level teasp. ground ginger*
4 *oz. cooking fat*	1 *egg*
3 *oz. castor sugar*	2 *tbs. apricot or gooseberry jam*

Icing

4 *oz. icing sugar*	*crystallized ginger*
warm water	

Heat an oven to 350° F. (No. 4 in a gas oven) and grease a 7″ sandwich-tin. Sieve the flour and ground ginger and rub in the fat. Add the castor sugar and bind with the egg. Turn on to a lightly floured surface and divide in half. Knead each piece and roll to a circle, 7″ in diameter. Place one circle in the tin and spread with jam to ¼″ from the edge. Place the other circle on top and bake in the oven 50–55 minutes. Turn on to a wire tray, using the circle next the base of the tin as the top. When cold, ice the top with glacé icing and decorate with slices of crystallized ginger.

GINGER SNAPS

6 oz. self-raising flour
1 level teasp. bicarbonate of soda
2 oz. margarine
4 oz. castor sugar

1 level teasp. ground ginger
1½ oz. syrup
½ egg

Cream the margarine, sugar and syrup and work in the egg
and dry ingredients. Form into a sausage shape and cut into
36 pieces. Roll each into a ball, between the hands, and place
½″ apart on a lightly greased tray. Bake in an oven heated to
350° F. (No. 4 in a gas oven) for 15–20 minutes. Cool on a
wire tray and store in a biscuit-tin with a tight-fitting lid.

MELTING MOMENTS

8 oz. cornflour
2 level teasp. baking powder
6 oz. butter

2 eggs
grated rind of ½ lemon
3 oz. castor sugar

Lightly grease two dozen deep patty tins. Cream the butter
and sugar and work in the finely grated lemon rind. Beat the
eggs in a small basin and beat them into the mixture, adding
1 teasp. cornflour with each egg. Stir in the rest of the cornflour and the baking powder. Half fill the patty tins with the
mixture. Bake in an oven heated to 400° F. (No. 6 in a gas
oven) for 12–15 minutes. Cool on a wire tray.

MORNING ROLLS

½ lb. flour
1 level teasp. salt
1 oz. margarine or lard

½ oz. yeast
¼ pint warm milk

Sieve the flour and salt and rub in the margarine. Crumble the yeast into the warm milk and mix to a soft dough. Place the bowl in a polythene bag and leave to rise in a warm place to double its size. Turn on to a floured working surface and knead well. Divide into 6 equal pieces. Roll each piece under the hand till smooth and place on a greased tray, pressing to a flat round shape. Cover with the polythene bag and leave in a warm place for 15 minutes. Dust with flour and bake 15 minutes in an oven heated to 430° F.

If dried yeast is preferred, use only $\frac{1}{4}$ oz. Place the yeast in the warm milk and leave approximately 10 minutes till the surface is covered with bubbles, then proceed as before.

If required fresh for breakfast, make up the dough using only $\frac{1}{4}$ oz. fresh yeast and leave overnight in the polythene bag in the refrigerator. Next morning, knead, shape, prove and bake the rolls.

OATCAKES—THICK

8 *oz. medium oatmeal*
4 *oz. flour*
1 *level teasp. salt*
2 *level teasp. baking powder*

2 *level teasp. sugar*
3 *oz. margarine or cooking fat*
4 *tbs. cold water*

Sieve the flour, salt and baking powder into a bowl and add the oatmeal and sugar. Rub in the fat. Mix with water to a firm consistency. Knead lightly on a surface sprinkled with oatmeal. Roll out $\frac{1}{4}''$ thick and cut into rounds. Bake 15 minutes in an oven heated to 350° F. (No. 4 in a gas oven). Cool on a wire tray. Serve with butter and cheese or use as a base for a cold savoury topping.

OATCAKES—THIN

2 oz. medium oatmeal
2 oz. fine oatmeal
½ level teasp. salt

pinch of bicarbonate of soda
1 dsp. melted bacon fat
4 tbs. hot water

Mix together the medium and fine oatmeal, the salt and bicarbonate of soda and add the fat. Using a wooden spoon, mix with the water to a soft consistency. Turn on to a board, sprinkled liberally with fine oatmeal and press out to a circle using the knuckle of the right hand. Roll as thinly as possible and rub over with oatmeal to whiten. Brush off the surplus oatmeal and cut into 4. Place on a hot girdle and bake 5 minutes till cooked on the underside but not coloured. Crisp in a hot oven or before the fire.

To test the heat of a girdle, place the palm of the hand ½″ above it. If a comfortable heat is given off, the girdle is moderately hot. Sharper heat indicates too hot a girdle.

OATMEAL BISCUITS

4 oz. flour
2 oz. medium oatmeal
2 oz. fine oatmeal
pinch of salt
2 level teasp. baking powder

1 oz. margarine
1 oz. cooking fat
2 oz. castor sugar
1 egg
2 tbs. milk

To make the biscuits, mix together the flour, oatmeal, salt and baking powder. Rub in the fats and add the sugar. Bind with the beaten egg and milk. Knead lightly and roll out ¼″ thick. Cut into circles using a 2½″ plain round cutter. Place on a lightly greased tray and prick. Bake 15–20 minutes in an oven heated to 350° F. (No. 4 in a gas oven). Cool and store in a biscuit-tin with a tight lid.

PARKINS

4 oz. flour	1½ level teasp. bicarbonate of soda
2 oz. medium oatmeal	1 level teasp. ground ginger
2 oz. margarine	1 level teasp. ground cinnamon
2 oz. castor sugar	2 oz. syrup
10 almonds skinned	2 teasp. vinegar

Heat an oven to 350° F. and grease a tray lightly. Split the almonds in half. Rub the margarine into the sieved flour and spices, add the oatmeal and sugar. Stir the bicarbonate of soda and vinegar together and add to the dry ingredients with the syrup. Mix well. Turn on to a lightly floured working surface and form a roll. Cut into 20. Shape each piece to a ball and flatten on the tray. Put a half almond in the centre of each biscuit and bake approximately 20 minutes in the centre of the oven. Cool on a wire tray and store in an airtight tin.

PARLIAMENT CAKES

½ lb. flour	¼ lb. treacle
¼ lb. mixed fats	2 level teasp. ground ginger
¼ lb. moist brown sugar	

Sieve the flour and ground ginger and add the sugar. Melt the fat, add the treacle and bring to the boil. Pour over the dry ingredients and mix quickly with a wooden spoon. When smooth, turn on to a lightly greased, shallow baking-tray and roll out ⅛″ in thickness. Mark in 3″ squares and prick all over. Bake in an oven at 300° F. (No. 2 in a gas oven) for 20–30 minutes. When dark brown but still soft, place on a wire tray to cool and become crisp.

PETTICOAT TAILS

4 *oz. flour*
2 *oz. rice flour*

4 *oz. butter*
2 *oz. castor sugar*

Sieve the dry ingredients on to a working surface. Place the butter in the centre and gradually work the ingredients together with the hand until bound but not soft and oily. Roll into a circle approximately 8″ in diameter and place on a baking-tray. Using a plain 3″ round cutter, cut a circle in the middle. Do not remove. Cut the outer ring into 8 segments. These form the petticoat tails. Bake in the centre of an oven, heated to 300° F. for 20–30 minutes. When cooked and very lightly coloured, dust with castor sugar, cool on a wire tray and serve on a plate in the shape of the original cake.

Note: 1. 6 oz. flour may be used instead of 4 oz. flour and 2 oz. rice flour.

2. If preferred, knead the ingredients in a bowl and then roll out on the working surface.

PITCAITHLY BANNOCK

8 *oz. flour*
4 *oz. butter*
2 *oz. castor sugar*

1 *oz. blanched almonds*
1 *oz. peel, orange or citron*

Remove the skins from the almonds and chop finely. Mix with the finely chopped peel. Knead the butter and sugar by hand on a wooden surface rather than in a bowl. Sieve the flour and work it into the butter with the peel and almonds. Knead till smooth. Press with the hand into a round cake ½″–¾″ thick or shape in a mould dusted with rice flour. It will be about 8″ across. Lay on a baking-tray covered with lightly greased paper. Prick all over with a fork or skewer. Cook in the middle of an oven heated to 320° F. (No. 3 in a gas oven) and bake 45–50 minutes till lightly coloured and cooked to the centre. Sprinkle with castor sugar and cool slightly on the tray before placing on a wire tray.

QUEEN CAKES

6 oz. flour
2 level teasp. baking powder
4 oz. butter or margarine
2 oz. currants

4 oz. castor sugar
2 large eggs
approx. ½ tbs. milk or water

Grease 18 fluted queen cake-tins and place a ring of currants in the foot of each to form the crown. Cream the fat and sugar until soft and light, beat in the eggs, one at a time, adding 1 teasp. flour with each if the mixture shows signs of curdling. Stir in the flour sieved with the baking powder. Add enough milk or water to make a soft dropping consistency. Divide the mixture between the tins and bake 15–20 minutes in an oven heated to 400° F. (No. 6 in a gas oven). Remove from the tins and cool on a wire tray.

QUEEN MARY TARTLETS

Pastry
4 oz. flour
pinch of salt
2½ oz. margarine or mixture of
        fats
½ level teasp. sugar
1 yolk of egg
2 teasp. cold water

Filling
2 oz. margarine or butter
2 oz. castor sugar
1 egg
4 oz. sultanas
1 oz. mixed peel

To make the pastry, sieve the flour and salt, rub in the fat and add the sugar. Mix with the yolk of egg and water. Roll out thinly, cut into circles and line 10–12 tartlet tins.

To prepare the filling, cream the margarine and sugar and beat in the egg. Stir in the sultanas and peel. Divide the mixture between the tartlet tins. Bake 30–35 minutes in an oven heated to 375° F. (No. 5 in a gas oven). When the pastry is cooked under the filling, cool on a wire tray.

SEED CAKE

½ *lb. flour*	1 *oz. caraway seeds*
2 *level teasp. baking powder*	3 *oz. mixed peel*
6 *oz. butter*	2 *eggs*
6 *oz. castor sugar*	1 *tbs. water*

Line a round 6″ cake-tin with greased paper, and sieve the flour and baking powder. Cream the butter and sugar till light and beat in the eggs. Stir in the flour, caraway seeds, mixed peel and water and turn into the cake-tin. Bake in the centre of an oven heated to 330° F. for 1¼–1½ hours.

SPONGE CAKE

3 *oz. flour*	3 *large eggs*
4½ *oz. castor sugar*	

Heat an oven to 350° F. (No. 4 in a gas oven). Grease two 8″ sandwich-tins and put a circle of greased paper in the foot of each tin. Dust the tins with equal quantities of rice flour and castor sugar if a crisp crust is desired. Break the eggs into a large basin and add the sugar. Place the basin over a pan of hot water and whisk till light and frothy, or whisk in an electric mixer. Remove from the pan and whisk till cool. Lightly fold in the flour, which has been dried and sieved and divide the mixture evenly between the tins. Bake 20 minutes in the middle of the oven till risen, spongy and light brown in colour. Cool on a wire tray. Spread one cake with whipped cream and the other with fresh berried fruits or jelly and sandwich together. Dust the top with icing sugar.

SPONGE GINGERBREAD

1 *lb. flour*	½ *lb. castor sugar*
2 *level teasp. bicarbonate of soda*	½ *lb. syrup*
2 *teasp. vinegar*	1 *dsp. ground ginger*
2 *oz. margarine*	1 *egg*
2 *oz. cooking fat*	½ *pint milk*

Grease and line a flat tin 10″ × 8″ × 2″. Heat the margarine, fat, sugar and syrup till the fat is melted. Sieve the flour and ginger and add the ingredients from the pan along with the egg and milk. Moisten the bicarbonate of soda with the vinegar and add to the mixture. Beat till smooth, then pour into the prepared tin. Place in the centre of an oven heated to 330° F. (No. 3 in a gas oven). Bake approximately 1 hour. Remove the paper and cool.

SCONES

BARLEY MEAL SCONES

4 *oz. flour*	2 *level teasp. cream of tartar*
4 *oz. barley meal*	1½ *oz. margarine or butter*
½ *level teasp. salt*	¼ *pint milk*
1 *level teasp. bicarbonate of soda*	

Sieve the flour, salt and raising agents and add the barley meal. Rub in the margarine and mix with milk to a soft dough. Knead very lightly on a working surface and when smooth on the underside turn over and roll into a circle ½″

thick. Place on a baking-tray and cut into eight; brush with milk. If preferred, roll $\frac{1}{2}''$ thick and cut into individual round scones. Bake 10–12 minutes in an oven heated to 430° F. (No. 8 in a gas oven). Cool on a wire tray. If a smoother scone is preferred, use barley flour, or if a rougher scone is desired, use barley meal.

BROWN SCONES

4 oz. flour	2 level teasp. cream of tartar
4 oz. wheat meal	1½ oz. margarine or butter
½ level teasp. salt	¼ pint milk
1 level teasp. bicarbonate of soda	

Sieve the flour, salt and raising agents. Add the wheat meal and rub in the margarine. Mix to a soft consistency with the milk. Knead very lightly on a working surface until smooth. Roll to $\frac{1}{2}''$ in thickness and cut into individual scones or into two circles $\frac{1}{2}''$ thick and cut into quarters. Place on a baking-tray and brush with milk. Bake 10–12 minutes in an oven heated to 430° F. (No. 8 in a gas oven). When cooked, cool on a wire tray.

CHEESE SCONES

8 oz. flour	1½ oz. margarine
½ level teasp. salt	3 oz. grated cheese
1 level teasp. bicarbonate of soda	large pinch of cayenne pepper
2 level teasp. cream of tartar	¼ pint milk

Sieve together the dry ingredients, rub in the margarine and add the cheese. Mix with milk to a soft elastic dough. Knead very lightly on a working surface and roll out $\frac{1}{2}''$ thick. Cut into rounds or ovals, lay on a baking-tray and brush the top with milk. Bake 10–12 minutes at 430° F. (No. 8 in a gas oven). Cool on a wire tray.

Note: These are very popular split, buttered and served as simple open sandwiches, with a slice of tomato, cucumber, hard-boiled egg, etc., on top.

DROPPED SCONES

4 *oz. flour*
1 *level teasp. bicarbonate of soda*
2 *level teasp. cream of tartar*
1 *teasp. melted margarine or butter*

2 *level tbs. castor sugar*
1 *large egg*
6 *tbs. milk*

Heat a girdle slowly to ensure even heat throughout. Sieve the flour and raising agents and add the sugar and melted fat. Add the egg and milk and beat with a wooden spoon till smooth. When the girdle is hot, grease with a piece of suet on a fork or fat in a screw of paper. Pour the batter from the point of a dessertspoon on to the girdle. When the bubbles form on the surface turn the scones. Cook on the second side till brown and cooked to the centre. Cool in a towel on a wire tray. The mixture should be soft enough to drop off the spoon and find its own level, but at the same time should be firm enough to keep a good round shape.

OATMEAL SCONES

6 *oz. flour*
2 *oz. medium oatmeal*
¼ *level teasp. salt*
1 *level teasp. bicarbonate of soda*

2 *level teasp. cream of tartar*
1½ *oz. margarine or butter*
¼ *pint milk*

Sieve the flour, salt and raising agents, add the oatmeal and rub in the margarine. Mix with the milk to a soft consistency and turn on to a lightly floured working surface. Knead quickly and, when smooth, roll out ½″ in thickness. Cut into rounds and place on a baking-tray. Brush over the top with milk. Bake in an oven heated to 430° F. (No. 8 in a gas oven) for 10–12 minutes. Cool on a wire tray.

Note: If a smoother scone is desired, use fine instead of medium oatmeal.

POTATO SCONES

8 *oz. cooked sieved potato* ¼ *level teasp. salt*
2 *oz. flour* ½ *oz. margarine or butter*

Cream the margarine lightly and work in the potato. This is done more easily if the potato is still slightly warm. Add the salt and enough flour to make a soft, dry consistency. Knead lightly on a floured working surface till smooth and roll into a circle, as thin as possible. Divide into 8 or, if preferred, use a pot lid 4–5″ in diameter and cut into circles. Prick all over. Bake 2–3 minutes on a hot girdle and, when brown, turn over and bake 2–3 minutes on the second side. Cool in a towel or spread with butter, roll up, and serve at once. If any scones are left over, fry with bacon for breakfast.

TEA SCONES

8 *oz. flour* 1 *level teasp. bicarbonate of soda*
¼ *level teasp. salt* 2 *level teasp. cream of tartar*
1½ *oz. margarine or butter* ¼ *pint milk*

Sieve together the dry ingredients and rub in the margarine. Add all the milk at once and mix to a soft consistency. Turn on to a floured board and knead very lightly till smooth. Roll ½″ in thickness and cut out. Lay on a baking-tray and brush over the top with milk. Bake in an oven heated to 430° F. (No. 8 in a gas oven) for 10–12 minutes. Cool on a wire tray. If using a girdle, roll ¼″ in thickness before cutting. Lay on the moderately hot girdle and bake 3–4 minutes till brown on the underside, turn and cook 4–5 minutes. Cool in a towel on a wire tray. These scones can also be made using either 8 oz. plain flour and 2 level teasp. baking powder or 8 oz. self-raising flour.

TREACLE SCONES

8 oz. flour
pinch salt
1 level teasp. bicarbonate of soda
1 level teasp. cream of tartar
1½ oz. margarine
1 oz. castor sugar

1 level teasp. ground ginger
½ level teasp. ground cinnamon
½ level teasp. mixed spice
1 tbs. melted treacle
6 tbs. milk

Sieve the flour, salt, raising agents and the spices. Rub in the margarine and add the sugar. Mix to a stiff consistency with the treacle and milk and turn on to a lightly floured working surface. Knead lightly and, if to be baked in the oven, roll ½″ thick, or if to be baked on the girdle, ¼″ thick. Cut into 8 pieces, place on a baking-tray and bake 10–12 minutes in an oven heated to 400° F. or place on a moderately hot girdle. Bake 3–4 minutes on the first side and when brown, turn and bake 5–6 minutes on the second side. Cool on a wire tray if oven scones and in a towel on the tray if girdle scones.

Jams and Jellies

JAMS AND JELLIES

Soft fruits from the gardens, the field, the hedgerows and the wood, ripened slowly in the long days of summer, were made into jams and jellies unsurpassed in flavour. These were combined with sugar, from the West Indies, brought into the ports on the Clyde.

BLAEBERRY JAM

2 *lb. blaeberries*
1½ *lb. sugar*

juice of 1 *lemon or*
1 *teasp. tartaric acid*

Remove leaves and stalks from the fruit, wash in a colander and drain. Put in a pan, crush with a wooden spoon and add the lemon juice or the tartaric acid. Simmer until the fruit is soft and thick. Add the warmed sugar, allow to dissolve, then bring to the boil. Simmer for 40 minutes. Pour into clean hot jars and cover at once. This jam does not set to a jelly.

BRAMBLE JELLY

5 *lb. brambles*
1 *lb. cooking apples*

sugar
2 *pints water*

Wash the fruit after removing any stalks and leaves and cut up the apples roughly. Put the brambles, apples and water into a preserving pan and simmer until completely softened. Strain the mixture through a jelly bag and measure the juice. Return the juice to the pan, adding 1 lb. sugar to 1 pint juice. Stir till boiling and boil rapidly till setting point is reached in about 10–15 minutes. Remove any scum, cool very slightly and pour into warmed jelly jars. Cover and label.

If using a thermometer boil to 220° F.

A scalded linen cloth or tea towel makes a satisfactory jelly cloth.

CRANBERRY JELLY

cranberries   *water*
sugar

Wash the berries and put into a pan with barely enough water to cover. Simmer slowly until the berries are soft. This will take approximately ¾ hour. Strain through a jelly cloth. Measure the juice and return to the pan with 1 lb. sugar to 1 pint juice. Bring to the boil and boil rapidly until setting point is reached in about 15–20 minutes. Remove the scum, pour into jars, cover and label.

This makes an excellent accompaniment to roast game birds, roast turkey and venison.

GOOSEBERRY JAM

3 *lb. gooseberries*   6 *lb. sugar*
2 *pints water*

Wash, top and tail the gooseberries and put into a preserving pan with the water. Bring to the boil and simmer slowly till the skins are quite soft, from 30–40 minutes. Add the sugar, stir till boiling and cook quickly till setting point is reached. If using a thermometer boil to 220° F. Skim if necessary, pour into heated jars, cover and label. (10 lb. jam.)

GOOSEBERRY JELLY

4 lb. gooseberries   sugar
2–3 pints water

Wash the fruit and simmer gently in a pan with the water till the skins are soft and the fruit pulped. Strain through a jelly bag or a clean linen towel tied to the underside of a chair. Measure the juice and return to the rinsed pan. Add the sugar, allowing 1 lb. sugar to 1 pint juice. Stir till boiling and cook quickly till setting point is reached. Cool slightly, skim if necessary and pour into heated jelly jars. Cover and label.

MARMALADE—DARK

3 lb. Seville oranges   sugar
3 lemons   7 pints water
                            1 oz. black treacle

Wash the fruit thoroughly, peel off the rind and cut in shreds or mince roughly. Cut up the fruit, remove the pips and tie in muslin. Soak rind, fruit and pips in water overnight. Put into a preserving pan and simmer 1–1¼ hours till the rind is soft. Remove the muslin bag, squeezing out all the liquid. Measure the pulp and return to the pan with the treacle and the sugar, allowing 1 lb. sugar to 1 pint pulp. Stir till boiling and boil rapidly for approximately 20 minutes or until setting point is reached. If using a thermometer boil to 220° F. Skim, cool slightly, pour into heated jars, cover and label.

MARMALADE—DUNDEE

3 *lb. Seville oranges*   6 *lb. sugar*
3 *lemons*   6 *pints water*

Wash the fruit, put into a pan with the water and put on the lid. Bring to the boil and simmer till the fruit is soft, then cut into small pieces. Remove the pips and simmer 15 minutes in the juice, then strain. Put the fruit, juice and sugar into a pan, stir till boiling, then boil rapidly till setting point is reached—about 20 minutes. Remove any scum, cool slightly, pour into heated jars, cover and label. (10 lb.)

MARMALADE—JELLY

4 *lb. Seville oranges*   *sugar*
2 *lemons*   *water*

Wash the fruit thoroughly. Remove a thin rind from the oranges and cut into 1″ chips. Soak overnight in 1 pint of water and then simmer till soft. Cut up the fruit and soak overnight in enough water to cover. Strain the water from the chips and add to the fruit. Put into a preserving pan and simmer till tender for 1–1½ hours. Strain through a jelly cloth. Measure the liquid and return to the pan with 1 lb. sugar to 1 pint juice and the chips. Stir till boiling and boil rapidly to 220° F. or setting point if no thermometer is available. Skim, cool slightly, pour into heated jelly jars, cover and label.

MARMALADE—QUICKLY MADE

1 *lb. Seville oranges*   4 *lb. sugar*
1 *lemon*   4 *pints water*

Wash the oranges and lemon and cut into eighths. Remove the pips and tie in muslin. Mince the fruit and put into a preserving pan with the water and muslin bag. Bring to the boil and simmer 1 hour. Remove the muslin bag, pressing as much liquid from it as possible. Add the sugar, stir till boiling and boil rapidly till setting point is reached, in about ½ hour. Remove any scum, cool slightly and pour into warm jars. Cover and label. (About 7 lb.)

MARMALADE—THREE FRUIT

2 *grapefruit*	5 *pints water*
4 *lemons*	6 *lb. sugar*
2 *oranges*	

Wash the fruit and remove the peel. Cut away the pith from the peel. Cut the flesh of the fruit into pieces and remove the pips. Tie the pith and pips in a muslin bag. Cut the peel into shreds. Put the fruit, shreds, muslin bag and water into a preserving pan and simmer till the peel is quite soft. Remove the muslin bag, squeezing from it as much juice as possible and add the sugar. Stir till boiling and boil rapidly till setting point is reached. Remove any scum, cool slightly, then pour into warmed jars. Cover and label. (10 lb.)

RASPBERRY JAM

6 *lb. raspberries*   6 *lb. sugar*

Put the prepared fruit into a preserving pan and heat very slowly. Simmer gently until the fruit is soft, approximately 10 minutes. Add the sugar, stir till boiling and boil rapidly 3 minutes. Remove any scum, pot, cover and label. (10 lb.)

RHUBARB JAM

7 *lb. rhubarb*
7 *lb. sugar*
juice of 1 *lemon*

4 *oz. crystallized ginger*
1 *oz. root ginger*

Prepare the rhubarb and cut into 1" lengths. Chop the crystallized ginger into small pieces. Bruise the root ginger and tie in muslin. Put all the ingredients into a basin and leave for 3 days. Turn into a preserving pan, bring to the boil and boil rapidly till setting point is reached. If a thermometer is used, boil to 220° F. Remove the muslin bag and pour into hot, clean jars. Cover closely with a wax cover and then a parchment or cellophane cover. Label. (Almost 11¾ lb.)

ROWAN JELLY

3 *lb. rowans*
1 *lb. apples*

sugar
water

Remove the stalks from the rowans and wash the berries. Wash the apples and cut up roughly. Put the fruits into a preserving pan with sufficient water to cover and simmer till the fruit is soft, approximately ¾ hour. Strain through a jelly cloth and measure the juice. Return to the pan with 1 lb. sugar to 1 pint of juice. Stir till boiling and boil rapidly till setting point is reached. Remove any scum and pour into small, warm jars. Cover and label. This makes a tart jelly, very suitable to serve with venison or mutton.

STRAWBERRY CONSERVE

4 *lb. hulled strawberries*

4 *lb. sugar*

Put strawberries and sugar in layers in a basin. Leave 24 hours. Boil for 5 minutes in a suitable sized pan. Return to the basin and stand for 48 hours. Cook once more in a pan, boiling for 20 minutes or until setting point is reached. Cool slightly. Pour into small warmed jars, cover and label.

STRAWBERRY JAM

4 *lb. strawberries*
3½ *lb. sugar*

juice of 2 lemons or
½ *pint redcurrant juice*

Choose small berries as jam containing the whole fruit is the most popular. After hulling put the berries and lemon juice or redcurrant juice into a pan and heat slowly till the juice runs and the fruit softens. This will take 15–20 minutes. Add the sugar, stir till boiling and boil rapidly till setting point is reached, 220° F. if a thermometer is used. Remove scum and allow the jam to begin to set slightly in the pan to prevent the berries rising to the top of the jars. Pour into heated jars, cover and label. (About 6 lb.)

Sweets

SWEETS

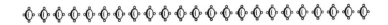

'Taiblet's awfie guid'—J. J. Bell

BUTTERSCOTCH

¾ *lb. demerara sugar*
¼ *lb. glucose*

3 *oz. unsalted butter or margarine*
¼ *pint water*

Dissolve the sugar slowly in the water and add the glucose. Stir in the fat in small pats and bring to the boil. Boil, without stirring, to 280° F. brushing down the sides of the pan when necessary. Pour into an oiled tin. Mark when setting and cut into squares. Wrap in waxed paper and store in a jar or tin with a tight-fitting lid.

The brush must be damp but not wet when brushing down syrup. It is essential to use a thermometer for this toffee.

CARAMEL WALNUTS

Marzipan made from:
½ *lb. granulated sugar*
½ *gill water*
pinch of cream of tartar
2 *small yolks of eggs*
6 *oz. ground almonds*
walnut halves

Syrup made from:
½ *lb. granulated sugar*
1 *gill water*
pinch of cream of tartar

Make the marzipan by putting the water and sugar into a pan and heating slowly. When the sugar has dissolved, add the cream of tartar and boil to 240° F. Remove from the heat and stir in the ground almonds. Add the yolks of eggs, one at a time and cook slightly. Pour on to a working surface or marble slab dusted with icing sugar and, when sufficiently cool, knead with the fingers till smooth. Form into balls the size of a walnut and flatten slightly. Press a halved walnut on top or on each side. Set aside to dry for 5–6 hours or overnight.

Dissolve the sugar in the water for the syrup, add the cream of tartar and boil to 310° F. in a small, deep pan. Drop in the marzipan balls and coat with the syrup. Remove with oiled forks and allow to set on oiled plates before putting into sweet cases.

To give variety, colour part of the marzipan pink and part green, as well as leaving part uncoloured.

FUDGE

1 *lb. granulated sugar*   2 *oz. butter*
¼ *pint water*   1 *small tin condensed milk*

To make the fudge, dissolve the sugar in the water and strain. Return to the pan with the condensed milk and heat gently, stirring all the time. When dissolved, add the butter in small pats, being careful to see that one pat is thoroughly incorporated before adding the next. Bring to the boil and boil rapidly to 240° F.—soft ball. If any sugar crystallizes on the side of the pan during boiling, brush down with a brush dipped in hot water. Remove from the heat and allow the bubbles to subside. Flavour and beat till creamy and thick. Pour into an oiled tin 5″ × 10″ and mark when almost cold.

Use one of the following to vary the flavour:

1 *teasp. vanilla essence*	4 *oz. crystallized ginger*
2 *oz. grated chocolate*	1 *oz. raisins*, 1 *oz. chopped*
2 *teasp. instant coffee and*	*almonds and*
2 *oz. chopped walnuts*	¼ *teasp. almond essence*

HELENSBURGH TOFFEE

1 *lb. granulated sugar*	1 *small tin condensed milk*
2 *oz. butter*	4 *tbs. milk*
1 *dsp. syrup*	½ *teasp. vanilla essence*

Grease a tin 5″ × 10″. Into a pan put the milk and butter and allow to melt. Add the sugar and syrup and dissolve slowly, then pour in the condensed milk, stirring all the time. Boil to 240° F. stirring gently. Remove from the heat and allow to settle. Add sufficient vanilla essence to flavour. Beat well till thick and beginning to grain. Pour into the tin and mark into squares when almost set. If no thermometer is available, boil to the soft-ball stage. To test for this, place a small amount in cold water. This should feel like putty when rolled between the fingers.

VANILLA TABLET

1 *lb. granulated sugar*	¼ *pint milk*
2 *oz. butter*	1 *teasp. vanilla essence*
1 *tbs. syrup*	

Before making the tablet, grease a tin 6″ × 6″. Put the milk, sugar, butter and syrup into a pan and dissolve slowly. Boil to 245° F., or soft ball when tested in cold water, stirring all the time. Remove from the heat and allow the bubbles to settle, add the vanilla essence and beat till thick. Pour into the tin and mark when almost cold.

Vary the flavouring by adding one of the following:

4 *oz. walnuts*	2 *oz. crystallized ginger*
rind and juice of 1 *orange*	2 *tbs. coffee essence*
2 *teasp. cocoa*	

HUMBUGS

1 *lb. demerara sugar*	¼ *level teasp. cream of tartar*
1½ *oz. butter*	¼ *pint water*
1 *dsp. syrup*	3 *drops oil of peppermint*
1 *dsp. treacle*	

Put the water and sugar into a pan and dissolve slowly. Add the cream of tartar, the syrup and treacle and the butter in wafer-like slices. Stir till boiling and then remove the spoon. Brush down the sides of the pan if necessary. Boil to the crack, i.e. 290° F. Remove from the heat and allow the bubbles to subside and a thin skin to form. Oil a marble slab or strong enamel tray thoroughly and pour the mixture on to it. Add the oil of peppermint. Oil the hands well and when cool enough to handle pull the toffee till smooth, light in colour and beginning to stiffen. Pull to a long strip and cut in ½″ lengths with oiled scissors. Store in a tin or jar with a tight-fitting lid.

Puddings Hot and Cold

PUDDINGS HOT AND COLD

Puddings as a second course are not traditionally Scottish, although the savoury pudding has a firm national basis and appears in all the old recipe books. Sweet puddings grew in popularity during the eighteenth and early nineteenth centuries and seem to come from two sources.

The steamed pudding, the fruit pie and the filled tart originated south of the Border. They are essentially English and belong to traditional English cookery. The Cloutie Dumpling, however, sliced and served cold, has sustained many a working man through a long day. When served hot as it is turned out of the cloth, or sliced and fried and served dredged with sugar, the dumpling is a special occasion pudding.

The cold pudding owes much to French influence and most recipes are based on a custard base with sponge or ratafia biscuits to give substance. Fruit and cream give variety. Recipes which owe much to French patisserie are generally less elaborate than those served in France and these and the gâteaux based on French recipes appear at teatime rather than as a pudding.

Throughout Scotland the pudding appears regularly in present-day meals and the recipes vary from district to district but are based principally on ideas culled from France and England.

APPLE PLATE TART

Pastry

6 oz. flour
pinch salt
3 oz. margarine

½ oz. cooking fat
6 teasp. water

Filling

¼ lb. apples

2 oz. sugar

Sieve the flour and salt for the pastry and rub in the fats. Mix with water and turn on to a lightly floured working surface. Divide into two-thirds and one-third and knead each piece lightly. Roll the larger piece to a circle to fit a 6″ plate, allowing ½″ to come beyond the edge. Roll the smaller piece to a strip and cut in lengths of unequal length and ½″ wide. Form these into a close trellis on a piece of greaseproof paper. Prepare the apples and cut in thin slices. Wet the rim of the plate and fit on the circle of pastry. Put in the slices of apple and sugar. Wet the edge of the pastry and slide the trellis on top of the apples. Carefully fold over the edge of the circle on top of the trellis, knock up and make a biscuit edge. Bake 30–35 minutes in an oven heated to 375° F., reducing the heat to 350° F. when the pastry has set and begun to colour. Serve hot or cold accompanied by cream.

AULD MAN'S MILK

3 eggs
1 pint milk or thin cream
1 sherry glass sherry or brandy
1 sherry glass whisky or rum

4 oz. loaf sugar
1 lemon
nutmeg

Rub the lemon rind with the loaf sugar to remove the zest, put the sugar in a bowl with the alcohol and leave to dissolve.

Separate the eggs, beat the yolks and add the sugar mixture and the milk or cream. Beat the whites till stiff and add to the mixture. Flavour with nutmeg or lemon juice if a sharper flavour is liked. Serve in large custard glasses as a nourishing drink.

AUNT MARY'S PUDDING

4 oz. breadcrumbs	4 oz. brown sugar
4 oz. stoned raisins	4 eggs
4 oz. currants	1 level teasp. ground ginger
4 oz. chopped apples	½ level teasp. grated nutmeg
1 sherry glass brandy	½ level teasp. salt

Mix all the ingredients together and steam in a well-greased basin for 3 hours.

Serve with a thin cornflour sauce, well flavoured with brandy and nutmeg.

BRAMBLE AND APPLE FOOL

1 lb. brambles	¼ pint water
¾ lb. apples weighed after peeling	½ pint cream (double)
½ lemon	6 oz. sugar

Wash and pick over the brambles and cook to a pulp with the apples, sugar, water and rind and juice of the lemon. Remove the lemon rind and then sieve the mixture or put into the liquidizer until smooth. Test the pulp for flavour and sweeten as required. Half whip the cream and when it begins to thicken, beat in the fruit pulp gradually. Put into a glass bowl and serve chilled with sponge fingers, boudoir biscuits or shortbread fingers.

BURNT CREAM (1)

1 *pint cream*
4 *egg yolks*
1 *oz. castor sugar*

1 *vanilla pod or*
½ *teasp. vanilla essence*
additional castor sugar

Heat the cream in a double saucepan. If a vanilla pod is used put it in the cream as it heats and remove when the cream is hot but not boiling. If essence is used, add when the cream is hot. Pour the hot cream on to the yolks of eggs well mixed with 1 oz. castor sugar. Return to the double pan and cook as for a cup custard. Do not overcook or the mixture will curdle. Pour into a shallow dish and leave overnight, then sprinkle the surface with castor sugar until there is an even coating rather less than ¼″ thick. Put the shallow dish into a grill pan and pack it round with ice. Put under a very hot grill and watch carefully as the sugar melts and caramels. Remove pan from the heat when the sugar is golden brown and chill well before serving.

BURNT CREAM (2)

4 *large eggs*
½ *pint milk*
½ *pint double cream*

2 *oz. castor sugar*
2 *oz. icing sugar*

Heat an oven to 280° F. (No. 1 in a gas oven). Put the milk and cream into a pan with a heavy base, or a double boiler, and heat very slowly till steaming. Beat together the eggs and castor sugar, add the hot milk and cream and strain into an oven-proof dish. Place in a tin containing hot water and bake in the centre of the oven for 1¼–1½ hours. When ready, the mixture will have set in the centre. When cool, sprinkle on the icing sugar to form a thick layer. Place under a hot grill till golden brown. Leave in a cool place for some hours before serving. If preferred, use demerara sugar in place of icing sugar.

CARAGEEN MOULD

½ oz. carageen
1½ pints milk

grated rind of 1 lemon
1 oz. sugar

Wash the carageen and soak in water for 10 minutes, then drain. Warm the milk and infuse with the lemon rind and sugar for 10 minutes. Pour on to the carageen, return all to the pan and simmer 20 minutes. Strain into a wetted china mould and leave till set. Turn out and serve with cream or fruit.

Carageen can be bought in packets at some chemists and grocers.

CORSTORPHINE CREAM

milk
moist sugar

cream
fresh fruit

Pour a quart of fresh milk into a large basin and leave overnight in a warm place till a curd has formed. Add a pint of fresh milk and leave overnight after mixing well. Beat well with enough moist sugar to sweeten. Serve with fresh fruit and cream. It should have a slightly sour flavour.

Rutherglen Ream is very similar.

CLOUTIE DUMPLING

4 oz. flour
4 oz. breadcrumbs
4 oz. prepared suet
4 oz. moist sugar
1 level teasp. bicarbonate of soda

4 oz. currants
4 oz. sultanas
4 oz. raisins
1 egg
ale or milk to mix

Mix the dry ingredients and the prepared fruit. Add the egg and sufficient ale to form a dropping consistency. Stir well. Scald a cloth and rub over the surface with flour. Place in a bowl. Pour in the mixture and gather up the cloth, making sure that the folds of the cloth are evenly distributed. Tie the cloth, allowing room for the pudding to swell. Place the pudding on an old plate on the base of a pan and cover with boiling water. Boil 2–3 hours, replenishing the water when necessary. When removing the cloth, care must be taken not to break the 'skin'. Serve with a suitable sauce.

The proportion of flour and breadcrumbs can be varied as desired. Oatmeal is sometimes used instead of breadcrumbs. The amount of fruit can also be varied.

If milk is used instead of ale for mixing, add spice to give flavour.

If the pudding is steamed instead of boiled, allow 3–4 hours.

CRAIL PUDDING

1 oz. margarine or butter	1 egg
1 oz. flour	½ pint milk
½ oz. sugar	ground cinnamon

Melt the margarine, add the flour to the pan and cook for 2–3 minutes. Cool and add the milk. Stir till smooth, return to the heat and stir till boiling. Simmer 7–10 minutes. Add the sugar and vanilla essence, if desired. Stir in the yolk of egg. Whisk the white stiffly and fold in to the mixture. Pour into a pie-dish and bake 30 minutes in an oven heated to 350° F. Sprinkle cinnamon on the surface before serving hot.

CREAM CROWDIE

½ pint double cream	2 oz. pinhead oatmeal
1–2 oz. castor sugar	rum to flavour
½ lb. fresh raspberries	

Toast the oatmeal in the oven or in a thick frying-pan until it is lightly browned and has acquired a nutty flavour. Whip the cream until it leaves a trail when the whisk is drawn across the surface, fold in the oatmeal and sweeten to taste. Flavour well with rum and fold in the raspberries.

The fruit may be omitted.

CROWDIE

1 *quart fresh or sour milk*	1 *tbs. cream*
½ *teasp. rennet*	*salt, pepper*

Heat the milk till tepid and pour into a bowl. Stir in the rennet and leave in a warm place till a curd has formed. Cut the curd into 1″ cubes and leave 10 minutes to allow the whey to separate. Run off as much whey as possible and put the curds into a piece of muslin. Tie tightly and hang up to drain. Retie if necessary. Stir in the seasoning and the cream and pack tightly into a basin. Turn out when set. Vary the flavour by the addition of caraway seeds, fresh herbs, chopped syboes, chopped walnuts or almonds.

CURDS AND CREAM

1 *pint milk*	1 *gill double cream*
1 *teasp. rennet*	2 *level teasp. castor sugar*
grated nutmeg	

Heat the milk to blood heat and pour into a glass dish. Gently stir in the rennet and leave in a warm place till set. Whisk up the cream and sugar and place on the curds. Grate over the top a small quantity of nutmeg. If liked, the curds can be sweetened and flavoured before the addition of the rennet.

DUNFILLAN PUDDING

4 oz. flour
pinch of salt
1½ oz. butter or margarine
2 oz. castor sugar
stewed fruit, e.g. apple, rhubarb,
    raspberries, brambles

1 level teasp. bicarbonate of soda
1 level teasp. cream of tartar
2 eggs
milk

Heat an oven to 350° F. and grease a pie-dish or casserole. Place the fruit in the base of the dish. Sieve the flour, salt and raising agents and rub in the fat. Add the sugar and the eggs and sufficient milk to make a soft consistency. Pour over the fruit and bake ½–¾ hour till well risen and spongy.

Many people prefer to increase the butter to 2 oz. and cream it with the sugar.

GROSET FOOL

1 lb. green gooseberries
⅛ pint water
8 oz. sugar

½ pint cream or ¼ pint cream and
¼ pint egg custard
2 sprigs of elder flowers

Wash the berries and cook till soft and pulpy with the water and sugar and elder flowers. Remove the flowers and rub the fruit through a nylon sieve. If the pulp is put into a liquidizer until smooth, it will go through the sieve very much more quickly. By itself, the liquidizer does not deal satisfactorily with the seeds which can only be removed by sieving. Half whip the cream and gradually add the fruit pulp, beating after each addition. If custard is used, add after the fruit. Test for sweetness; chill and serve with boudoir biscuits.

LEMON PUDDING

6 *egg yolks*   ½ *lb. sugar*
2 *egg whites*   ½ *lb. melted butter*
puff pastry   *juice and grated rind of* 1 *lemon*

Line a deep tin or plate with puff pastry. Bake the pastry blind and cool before filling. Beat the egg yolks and whites with the sugar, grated rind and juice of the lemon. When well mixed and frothy, stir in the melted butter. Pour into the pastry-case and bake for 30 minutes at 325° F. Serve cold, decorated with a sprinkling of coarse white sugar.

PLUM PUDDING

Based on Meg Dod's Recipe	*Based on Northern English Traditional Recipe*
4 *oz. breadcrumbs*	8 *oz. flour*
2 *oz. flour*	8 *oz. stoned raisins*
8 *oz. stoned raisins*	8 *oz. currants*
8 *oz. currants*	8 *oz. sultanas*
8 *oz. shredded suet*	8 *oz. shredded suet*
3 *oz. chopped mixed peel*	8 *oz. chopped mixed peel*
4 *oz. sugar*	8 *oz. brown sugar*
2 *oz. almonds, blanched and chopped*	4 *oz. almonds, blanched and chopped*
1 *level teasp. grated nutmeg*	1 *level teasp. grated nutmeg*
1 *level teasp. ground cinnamon*	1 *level teasp. ground cinnamon*
¼ *level teasp. ground mace*	1 *level teasp. mixed spice*
4 *eggs*	2–3 *eggs*
1 *sherry glass of brandy*	1 *glass rum, brandy or sherry*
milk	8 *oz. raw grated carrot or potato*

Mix all the ingredients together and put the mixture into well-greased pudding basins. The foil basins available now are excellent for this purpose. Cover carefully and leave room for the pudding to rise. Steam for 8 hours, cool and store in a dry place. If greaseproof paper or foil is used to cover, replace when the pudding is cold. Steam for 2–3 hours before using and serve with brandy or rum butter or a custard sauce, well flavoured with spice and rum or brandy. The puddings will keep for 12–18 months and improve in flavour as they mature.

This is the equivalent of the English Christmas Pudding and there is a strong resemblance between the recipes from the northern counties of England and those found in Scotland. There are two distinct types of recipe, one using raw potato or carrot, the other omitting vegetables. Another variation is the proportion of flour to crumbs (either bread or biscuit). Either recipe is equally good.

RHUBARB PLATE TART

Pastry

6 *oz. flour*   1 *yolk of egg*
4 *oz. mixed fats*   3 *teasp. water*
1 *level teasp. castor sugar*

Filling

½ *lb. rhubarb*   2–3 *oz. sugar*

Heat an oven to 400° F. Prepare the fruit and cut into ½″ lengths. Make the shortcrust pastry by rubbing the fats into the flour, adding the sugar and binding with the yolk of egg and water. Divide in two and roll out each half to a circle large enough to cover a 7″ plate. Wet the rim of the plate and place on a circle of pastry. Fill with the rhubarb and sugar, keeping as flat and smooth as possible. Wet the rim of pastry and cover the filling with the second circle of pastry. Knock up and flute the edges. Bake 10–15 minutes in the oven till the pastry has set, reduce the heat to 375° F. and leave till pastry and filling are cooked, 30–35 minutes. Sprinkle with castor sugar and serve hot or cold.

ROTHESAY PUDDING

4 oz. flour
4 oz. fresh breadcrumbs
4 oz. shredded suet
½ oz. castor sugar
3 tbs. raspberry jam

1 level teasp. bicarbonate of soda
1 teasp. vinegar
1 egg
¼ pint milk

Mix together all the dry ingredients except the bicarbonate of soda. Add the jam, beaten egg and milk. Stir the bicarbonate of soda into the vinegar and add to the other ingredients. Beat all together and pour into a greased basin, filling it not more than three-quarters full. Cover with a greased paper or foil and steam steadily for 2–2½ hours. Turn out and serve with a suitable sauce.

SCOTS TRIFLE

4 small sponge cakes
2 oz. ratafia biscuits
¼–½ pint mixture of fruit syrup
    and Drambuie
strawberry jam
Pistachio nuts and ratafia biscuits
    to decorate

Custard:
4 eggs
1 pint milk
1 oz. sugar
1 teasp. vanilla essence or ratafia
    essence
½ pint double cream
Drambuie to flavour the cream

Make the custard and cool. Split the sponge cakes and spread thickly with the jam. Cut up roughly and put in a glass dish. Add the ratafia biscuits, pour over the syrup and Drambuie and make sure there is enough liquid to make the base moist and full of flavour. Cover with the custard and leave to soak. Whip the cream, flavour with Drambuie to taste and spread all over the surface of the base. Decorate with chopped, shelled pistachio nuts and ratafias. Cherries and angelica are often used instead of pistachio nuts and ratafias. Sherry can be substituted for Drambuie.

SYLLABUB

½ *pint double cream*
1 *lemon*
¼ *lb. loaf sugar*

1 *glass sherry*
1 *glass brandy*

Rub the lemon with the loaf sugar until the zest is removed. Put the sugar, strained lemon juice, sherry and brandy into a bowl, allow the sugar to dissolve. Add the cream and whisk until a trail of cream is left across the surface when the whisk is drawn across. Put into individual glasses and chill for at least 2 hours before serving. This makes 6 portions.

URNEY PUDDING

4 *oz. flour*
4 *oz. margarine*
3 *oz. castor sugar*
2 *eggs*

1 *level teasp. bicarbonate of soda*
2 *tbs. strawberry jam* ·
1 *teasp. milk or water*

Prepare a pan of boiling water in which to steam the pudding and grease a basin. Sieve the flour. Cream the margarine and sugar thoroughly, beat in the eggs alternately with the flour.

Add the jam and bicarbonate of soda mixed with milk or water. Stir all the ingredients together and fill the greased basin not more than three-quarters full. Cover with greased paper or foil and steam steadily for 1½ hours approximately.

Index

INDEX